HAMLYN NATURE GUIDES

BIRDS
OF BRITAIN AND EUROPE

HAMLYN NATURE GUIDES
BIRDS
OF BRITAIN AND EUROPE
JOHN ANDREWS

HAMLYN

Acknowledgements

AQUILA PHOTOGRAPHICS: A. J. Bond 17C, 101T, D. Green 35B, H. A. Hems 87C, 93T + B, H. Kinloch 59B, 91T, 105C, T. Leach 27C, 83B. W. S. Paton 49C, 79T, J. L. Roberts 57B, D. Smith 59T, E. K. Thompson 99C, M. C. Wilkes 71C, 73B, 97C, 107B; ARDEA PHOTOGRAPHICS: 123T, Avon-Tilford 121T, J. A. Bailey 19B, 57T, 71T, 75T, 85T, 117T, R. J. C. Blewitt 31T, 55T, 65C, J. B. and S. Bottomley 19T, 41B, 43T, 47C, K. Carlson 59C, W. Curth 39C, 79B, M. D. England 73T, F. W. Fink 67T, M. E. J. Gore 109C, C. R. Knights 41C, 61C, 69C, 123C, P. Laub 37T, 49B, A. Lindau 45C, R. Richter 51B, 101B, S. Roberts 31B, B. L. Sage 67C, P. Steyn 33C, R. Vaughan 41T, 51C, 75B, J. Wightman 47B; F. V. BLACKBURN: 65B, 67B, 69T, 83T, 103B, 107C, 111C + B; R. J. C. BLEWITT: 63C, 85B; BRUCE COLEMAN LTD: 113B, E. Duscher 21T, 45B, 95C, G. Langsbury 45T, 51T, 79C, J. Markham 47T, Hans Reinhard 69B, S. C. Porter 57C, 109T; G. N. de FEU: ERIC HOSKING: 17T, 19C, 21B, 23C, 25C, 29B, 35T, 39B, 43C, 53T, 75C, 89T; JACANA: Chevalier 53C, Ducrot 77C, 111T, 115B, Dupont 63T, 125T, F. Henrion 115C, J. C. Maes 63B, P. Petit 29T, Robert 91C, 123B, R. Volot 73C, 117B; E. A. JANES: 99T, 103T; HOWARD LACEY: 37B; FRANK LANE: A. Christiansen 55B, 61T × B, N. Duerden 103C, Eichorn/Zingel 77B, F. Merlet 27B, 31C, N. Schrempp 89B, C. J. Smale 39T, R. Thompson 43B, 87B, 99B, D. Zingel 27T, 89C; NATURAL HISTORY PHOTOGRAPHIC AGENCY: A. Butler 97T, 119C, D. N. Dalton 21C, 81T, 85C, 95T, 119B, S. Dalton 15C + B. 17B, 55C, 71B, 93C, 95B, 105B, 113C, F. Greenway 49T, B. Hawkes 33B, 37C, E. A. Janes 97B, J. Jeffrey 15T, P. Scott 23B, 25T, 29C, 33T; ROYAL SOCIETY FOR THE PROTECTION OF BIRDS: 107T; J. WAGSTAFF: 65T; WILDLIFE STUDIES LTD: 23T, 25B, 35C, 53B, 77T, 81C + B, 83C, 87T, 91B, 101C, 105T, 109B, 113T, 115T, 117C, 119C, 121C + B, 125C + B.
Title page: Trevor Dolby.

First published 1978
This soft cover edition published 1988 by
The Hamlyn Publishing Group Ltd.,
now a Division of The Octopus Publishing Group plc,
Michelin House, 81 Fulham Road,
London SW3 6RB

Phototypeset by Photocomp Ltd   Printed by Mandarin Offset Hong Kong.

Contents

Introduction

This book is designed for the very many people who wish to identify easily and confidently the common or conspicuous birds that they see in their gardens, the countryside and on holiday. It covers only the more widespread and obvious species of northwest Europe, omitting those that are rare, have a very localized distribution, or are easily overlooked except by experienced ornithologists. 168 species are illustrated. The accompanying texts describe the distinctive features of their plumage, behaviour and voice, as well as summarizing when and where they are likely to be seen. In cases where two species are very similar in appearance and difficult to separate, special joint texts explain the points of difference between them.

In most bird books the species are arranged in a standard scientific order based on their evolutionary origins. This is useful in several ways, but not particularly helpful to someone who is new to the problems of bird identification. Here, the pictures and texts are arranged so that as far as possible birds that may be confused with each other are portrayed on the same, or adjacent, pages.

Bird indentification rapidly becomes easier with practice but at first even the common species will seem confusing. You will get a lot of help if you join a club or society and go on their outings. If you haven't the opportunity to do this, then concentrate initially on getting to know the birds that you see regularly around your home. When you know these twenty or thirty species fairly well and, given a reasonable view, can identify them quickly and confidently, they will provide a basis on which you can steadily extend your knowledge and identification skill.

Equipment

If you wish to identify more than the few species that you will see close to, you will need binoculars. Magnification should be by 8 or 10 times, but this is not the only factor to consider: cheap glasses with poor lenses may give poor performance. The best procedure is to go to a reputable binocular specialist and take his advice. You will be able to try out a wide variety of models and select one that best suits your requirements.

Telescopes are helpful for identifying birds far out at sea or on large water bodies, but they do not function well under poor light conditions and are heavy to carry around.

When and where to watch

Some birds are very tame and confiding, but most are wary and should be approached with caution. In woodland, most small birds may prove very hard to watch, and the best technique is to sit quietly with your back to a tree on the edge of a clearing and wait for the birds to come to you. Another good place to watch is at water, where all birds will eventually come to drink and bathe. Open waters, mudflats, and salt marshes on estuaries often hold large numbers of birds but because there is little cover, the nearer birds will flush as soon as you get close and their alarm may cause the whole area to empty. So take advantage of cover such as sea walls or bankside vegetation, and keep off the skyline. Cars make excellent 'hides' from which to watch birds and have the added merits of keeping you warm and dry.

The early morning is always a good time to watch. Singing and calling tend to be concentrated in the period after dawn, and birds are then on the move to their feeding places. The period before dusk is also an active time. Birds dislike wind and rain and prefer to keep in cover at such times. Wildfowl are likely to be found on open waters at any time during the day but waders' feeding rhythms are associated with the tides. At high tide, they are forced on to roosts where they may be easy to watch. Once the tide recedes, they move out to feed.

Respect birds' privacy at nesting time, be careful not to damage nests and vegetation as you go about your birdwatching, and obtain permission prior to crossing private land.

Colour and markings

Plumage coloration and pattern play an enormous part in identification. Fortunately, most common birds are so distinctive that, given a good view, you should have no problem in recognizing them. However, when faced with a new species, particularly if it has complex markings, it is sometimes difficult to know what to notice and remember. First, get the general impression of the bird's appearance — in fact, that is often all you will get, but it is frequently enough, especially as you have the invaluable aids of knowing where and when you have seen it, aids that will rule out at once many of the confusing possibilities.

If you are able to note details, look especially for any striking markings and check the extent of any blocks of colour. For instance, if the bird has a dark cap, does it extend below the eye or right down the back of the neck? If it has a coloured breast, does it extend up on to the cheeks or down to the belly? A remarkable number of small birds have stripes near the eye and their location and extent can be very helpful in separating some of the rather plain brown or greenish species, so note their size and position in relation to the eye. Many birds have white or pale wing bars and these, too, provide valuable clues; sometimes they will only become apparent when the bird is flushed and flies away, and at that time you should also be able to see any markings on the rump or tail. Beak and leg colour are especially important in some gulls and waders.

Size and shape

Size is obviously a helpful feature, and it may be useful to compare the bird with some nearby feature such as a plant. Birds at long range, at sea or in flight are very difficult to size accurately, but at least try to get an impression of relative proportions by comparing wing, body and head size with each other.

Shape is extremely important as it helps to narrow the choice straight away. Wildfowl, waders, gulls and woodpeckers are all cases in point, with a characteristic appearance which is extremely easy to recognize. As you look at them more closely, you will realize that many other birds also have distinctive shapes. Beak shape and length are often very helpful in identification. A hooked beak usually means the subject is a bird of prey. A long, probing beak indicates a wader, and the length of the beak relative to the size of the head may help considerably in distinguishing species such as redshank and ruff, which at times look similar. Ducks typically have a beak shape quite unlike that of other water birds such as grebes, moorhens and coots. Birds that feed on insects usually have slender, pointed bills and those that eat seeds have stout, rather conical bills. Noticing that feature alone helps enormously to narrow down the field among the many small birds of wood, hedgerow and undergrowth.

Leg length, too, can be extremely helpful, particularly in identifying waders, many of which look uniformly brownish in winter. If you have difficulty in judging the leg length, compare it with the size of the bird's body. Tail length and shape are also worth noting if they are in any way out of the ordinary – the adult swallows' tail streamers provide an obvious means of distinguishing them from swifts and martins, for example.

Behaviour and song

The lifestyles of many birds are very useful for identification purposes. For example, ducks such as mallard find their food on or close to the surface of the water and will up-end, but never dive. Others, like tufted ducks, feed on the bottom so they dive, but do not up-end. If you watch waders on the shore you will see that some species run busily around probing at random, whereas plovers always stand and watch for the telltale movement of a small creature before running forward to capture it.

Gait is also helpful. Most small birds hop when on the ground but some, such as pipits, wagtails and starlings walk or run, while others like larks and dunnocks often shuffle along. Quite a number of species, including tits, some warblers and finches, rarely descend on to the ground at all but have developed great agility among vegetation and will feed, hanging upside-down from a plant stem or treetop twig.

Flying style is always worth noting, even if it doesn't give you a precise identification. Some birds fly with consummate skill, while others, even quite closely related species, can differ considerably in this respect. Ravens are splendid aerobats, turning back-somersaults in flight, whereas crows are usually decorous plodders. Of course in most cases, the differences are less marked, but even with small birds significant variations may exist. Note whether they flap continuously, whether they intersperse flapping with glides, whether the flight is undulating or direct, and if it looks strong or feeble. You will quite quickly find that you are able to identify some species by flying style alone.

It is not easy to learn songs and calls but they are worthy of attention, because for many species they are quite characteristic. If you learn the most frequent and familiar calls, when you hear something new you will know that it is worth tracking down. The phonetic renderings of calls and songs given in books are of limited value and this book includes only those sounds which are most distinctive or helpful. It is a good practice, when you hear an unfamiliar call, to try and track down the bird that is making it and then write your own description of it or fit words to it. Note-making is always a good way of fixing new birds in your mind.

The combination of shape and behaviour is often enough by itself to identify a bird even if you see it only as a silhouette. Try comparing the mouse-like dunnock and the bouncy, cheerful house sparrow and you will quickly see that they have distinctive characteristics. This personal quality of a species is called its 'jizz'. Experienced bird-watchers rely greatly on this as well as on the area, habitat and season, all of which help to identify a bird seen only briefly, under conditions of bad light or in juvenile or adult plumages. Learning a bird's 'jizz' becomes increasingly easy with practice and is well worth the effort.

Habitats

Even the commonest birds do not occur everywhere. Some are restricted by range; quite a number of northwest European birds do not occur regularly in Ireland or in northern Scandinavia, while several that are common up to the French coast occur extremely rarely twenty-odd miles away across the Channel in Britain. Birds are also limited by habitat. A few species have the ability to exploit a wide variety of conditions, but most have special requirements that are only provided by a few types of habitat. For instance, tree pipits and meadow pipits look practically identical, but in the breeding season the latter will frequently be found on open, treeless moorland while the tree pipit's territory will certainly include trees or bushes. It is therefore very useful to know what a particular bird's habitat preferences are.

Many birds are migrants. Most insect-eating species leave northwest Europe in winter because there is little food available to them. Some others, notably wildfowl and waders, move from upland and Arctic breeding grounds to milder lowland and coastal situations.

The habitat tables

The following tables indicate the species which you are most likely to see in different habitats in the breeding season (S) and during the winter (W). There are two tables: one dealing with birds of sea and wetlands, and the other with birds of woods and open country. If you have seen a bird and are uncertain of its identity, you can refer to the relevant habitat in the tables and find out which birds are most likely to be there. Alternatively, if you are planning a trip to a new habitat, you can check in advance on the birds that live there.

Sea and wetlands

Species	Sea and estuarine waters	Cliffs and rocky coasts	Salt marshes and beaches	Lowland waters	Lowland marshes and reed beds	Upland waters	Page
Razorbill	S W	S					14
Guillemot	S W	S					14
Puffin	S W	S					14
Red-throated diver	S W					S	16
Cormorant	S W	S		W			16
Shag	S W	S					16
Grey heron			S W	S W	S W	S W	18
Bittern					S W		18
Great-crested grebe	W			S W			18
Little grebe				S W			20
Moorhen				S W	S W	S	20
Coot				S W		S	20
Tufted duck				S W			22
Pochard	W			S W			22
Goldeneye	W			W		S	22
Eider	S W						24
Wigeon	W		W	S W	W	S	24
Teal	W			S W	S W	S	24
Mallard	W			S W	S W	S W	26
Shoveler				S W	S W		26
Pintail				S W	S W	S	26
Red-breasted merganser	S W					S	28
Goosander				W		S W	28
Shelduck	S W		S W				28
Brent goose	W		W				30
Greylag goose				W	S W	S	30
Canada goose				S W	S W		30
Mute swan	W			S W	W		32
White stork					S		32
Gannet	S W	S					32
Great black-headed gull	S W	S W	S W	W			34
Lesser black-backed gull	S W	S W	S W	W			34
Herring gull	S W	S W	S W	S W			34
Common gull	S W	S W	S W	S W			34
Black-headed gull	S W	W	S W	S W	S W	S	36
Kittiwake	S W	S					36
Fulmar	S W	S					36
Common tern	S			S			38
Arctic tern	S						38
Black tern				S	S		38
Ringed plover			S W				38
Little ringed plover				S			38
Dunlin			W	W		S	40
Common sandpiper				S W		S	40
Green sandpiper			W				40
Grey plover			W				42
Golden plover					W	S	42
Knot			W				42
Snipe					S W	S	44
Ruff					S W		44
Redshank			S W	S W	S W		44
Curlew			S W		S W	S	46
Bar-tailed godwit			W				46
Black-tailed godwit			W		S W		46
Turnstone			S W			S	48
Oystercatcher			S W				48

Sea and wetlands

Species	Sea and estuarine waters	Cliffs and rocky coasts	Salt marshes and beaches	Lowland waters	Lowland marshes and reed beds	Upland waters	Page
Avocet			S W				48
Rock dove		S W					54
Short-eared owl			S W		S W		58
Marsh harrier					S		60
Montagu's harrier					S		60
Hen harrier			W		S W		60
Osprey				S		S	60
Kestrel		S W			S W		64
Peregrine falcon		W					66
Merlin		W					66
Raven		S W	S W		S W		74
Carrion/Hooded crow			S W		S W		74
Sand martin				S			78
Kingfisher				S W			82
Dipper						S W	82
Reed warbler					S		104
Marsh warbler					S		104
Sedge warbler					S		104
Grasshopper warbler					S		104
Reed bunting			W	S W	S W		118
Meadow pipit			W		S W		120
Rock pipit		S W		W	W	S W	120
Pied/White wagtail			W	S W	S W		124
Grey wagtail				S W		S W	124
Yellow/Blue-headed wagtail				S	S		124

Woodland and open country

Species	Broadleaved woodland	Conifer woodland	Scrub, young plantations, heaths	Parks and gardens	Farmland	Upland and moors	Page
Wigeon					W		24
Mallard					W		26
Pintail					W		26
Greylag goose					W		30
Canada goose				S	W		30
White stork				S			32
Lesser black-backed gull					W		34
Herring gull					W	S	34
Common gull					W	S	34
Black-headed gull					W	S	36
Dunlin						S	40
Golden plover					W	S	42
Snipe						S	44
Curlew						S	46
Turnstone						S	48
Lapwing					S W		50
Red/Willow grouse						S W	50
Black grouse			S W			S W	50

Woodland and open country

Species	Broadleaved woodland	Conifer woodland	Scrub, young plantations, heaths	Parks and gardens	Farmland	Upland and moors	Page
Pheasant	S W				S W		52
Grey partridge					S W		52
Red-legged partridge					S W		52
Wood pigeon	S W	S W			S W		54
Stock dove	S W				S W		54
Rock dove					S W		54
Turtle dove	S				S		56
Collared dove				S W			56
Little owl			S W		S W		56
Barn owl			S W		S W		58
Short-eared owl			S W		W	S W	58
Tawny owl	S W			S W			58
Montagu's harrier			S				60
Hen harrier			S W			S W	60
Golden eagle						S W	62
Buzzard	S W				S W	S W	62
Honey buzzard	S	S					62
Red kite	S W					S W	64
Kestrel	S W				S W	S W	64
Hobby			S		S		64
Peregrine falcon						S W	66
Merlin						S W	66
Sparrowhawk	S W	S W	S W		S W		66
Cuckoo	S	S	S		S	S	68
Nightjar			S				68
Wryneck	S						68
Green woodpecker	S W						70
Great spotted woodpecker	S W	S W					70
Lesser spotted woodpecker	S W						70
Golden oriole	S						72
Hoopoe			S		S		72
Jay	S W	S W					72
Raven	S W	S W	S W		S W	S W	74
Carrion/Hooded crow	S W	S W	S W		S W	S W	74
Rook	S W				S W		74
Jackdaw	S W	S W			S W		76
Magpie	S W	S W	S W		S W		76
Swift							
Swallow	Flying over all types of habitat, including wetlands						
House martin							
Great grey shrike			S W		S W	S	80
Lesser grey shrike			S		S		80
Red-backed shrike			S		S		80
Woodchat shrike			S		S		80
Waxwing		S	W	W			82
Mistle thrush	S W	S W			S W		84
Song thrush	S W	S W		S W	S W		84
Redwing	S	S		S	W		84
Fieldfare	S	S	S		W		86
Blackbird	S W	S W	S W	S W	S W		86
Ring ousel						S	86
Starling	S W	S W	S W	S W	S W	S W	88
Bluethroat	S	S					88

Woodland and open country

Species	Broadleaved woodland	Conifer woodland	Scrub, young plantations, heaths	Parks and gardens	Farmland	Upland and moors	Page
Robin	S W	S W	S W	S W	S W		88
Redstart	S			S			90
Nightingale	S		S				90
Stonechat			S W			S W	92
Whinchat			S			S	92
Wheatear			S			S	92
Spotted flycatcher	S	S					94
Pied flycatcher	S						94
Dunnock	S W	S W	S W	S W	S W		94
Wren	S W	S W	S W	S W	S W	S W	96
Nuthatch	S W						96
Treecreeper	S W	S W					96
Great tit	S W		W	S W	W		98
Blue tit	S W		W	S W	W		98
Long-tailed tit	S W	S W	S W	S W	S W		98
Coal tit	S W	S W					100
Crested tit		S W					100
Marsh tit	S W	S W	S W				100
Willow tit	S W	S W	S W				100
Blackcap	S		S				102
Garden warbler	S		S				102
Whitethroat			S		S		102
Lesser whitethroat	S		S				102
Grasshopper warbler			S				104
Dartford warbler			S W				106
Goldcrest	S W	S W	S W				106
Willow warbler	S		S				106
Chiffchaff	S						106
Wood warbler	S						108
Melodius warbler	S						108
Icterine warbler	S						108
Siskin	S W	S W					108
Serin	S W	S W	S W		S W		110
Greenfinch	S W		S W	S W	S W		110
Crossbill		S W					110
Goldfinch	S W		S W		S W		112
Linnet			S W		S W		112
Redpoll		S W	S W				112
Bullfinch	S W	S W	S W	S W	S W		114
Chaffinch	S W	S W	S W	S W	S W		114
Brambling	S W	S					114
Ortolan bunting			S	S			116
Yellowhammer			S W		S W		116
Cirl bunting			S W		S W		116
Reed bunting					S W		118
House sparrow	S W	S W	S W	S W	S W		118
Tree sparrow	S W	S W			W		118
Corn bunting					S W		120
Meadow pipit			S W			S	120
Tree pipit	S		S				120
Skylark			S W		S W		122
Woodlark			S W		S W		122
Crested lark			S W		S W		122
Pied/White wagtail					S W		124

Razorbill *Alca torda* L 41cm

The unmistakable feature of adult razorbills is the vertically flattened black beak with a white stripe across it. When out at sea the beak may be impossible to observe, but razorbills' upperparts are always black, whereas many guillemots look brown or greyish. Like other auks, razorbills fly fast with whirring wings, and as they usually fly low over the waves they are easily overlooked. Razorbills nest in colonies on rocky or cliff-faced coasts, laying a single large egg in a dark cleft or crevice. Often razorbills are found in association with both guillemots and puffins. Their breeding range extends from Brittany, through Britain and Ireland to Norway, and into the Baltic. At the end of the season adults and flightless young leave their colonies and live at sea; at this time the white plumage extends up to the lower face. By January the first arrivals are reappearing at the coast to breed again.

Guillemot *Uria aalge* L 42cm

In southerly colonies, guillemots are chocolate or greyish in colour, and easy to distinguish from razorbills even when the beak shape cannot be seen. In northern colonies the birds are darker, and there are more 'bridled' individuals with a white line surrounding, and running back from, the eye. Guillemots produce a single large egg, much tapered at one end so that it rolls in an arc, reducing the risk of its falling from the narrow cliff ledges on which the birds breed, crowded together, often in enormous numbers. They are found on the coasts of Spain and Portugal, in the British Isles and Norway and, like razorbills, move to sea as soon as the chick is old enough to swim, thus reducing the risk of predation by gulls and other birds. In summer plumage, the related black guillemot *(Cepphus grylle)* is black all over except for a white wing patch and red feet.

Puffin *Fratercula arctica* L 30cm

Puffins are easy to identify because of their enormous beaks which make them look very large-headed. In summer they have white faces, whereas both guillemots and razorbills have dark faces. However, young puffins are darker faced and have smaller beaks than adults, so confusion with other auks is possible. Puffins mostly nest in burrows which they excavate in the turf on undisturbed clifftops and islands. The colonies are often very large, and at times great numbers of birds may congregate in the sea close by. When the single chick is well grown but still flightless, its parents stop bringing it fish and hunger finally forces it to leave the burrow and make its way alone to the sea, usually under cover of darkness to avoid the large predatory gulls. Breeding on the French coast, in the British Isles and Norway, puffins mostly winter far out in the Atlantic.

Red-throated Diver *Gavia stellata* L 56cm

Male and female red-throated divers have red throats in summer, but these can look dark, so in bad light the uniformly brown back is the most reliable way of distinguishing them from black-throated divers *(Gavia arctica)* which have checked, black and white backs. Winter plumage of both species is brown above and pale below, but in this season the red-throated diver has much more white about the head; at all times the tip of the beak has a unique upward tilted look. Divers usually fly low on long, slender wings, and have a hump-backed appearance when in flight. Superbly adapted to their aquatic lives, they have a streamlined look quite unlike any duck, and in fact are barely able to walk on land. Feeding on fish, red-throated divers breed in Scotland and Scandinavia on small lakes (black-throated divers favour larger waters). They winter at sea and may be found off almost any part of the European coast.

Cormorant *Phalacrocorax carbo* L 90cm [middle]/**Shag** *Phalacrocorax aristotelis* L 75cm [bottom]

Cormorants and shags look rather alike, but can be separated by careful observation. Adult shags are black all over and at close range the plumage has a distinct greenish sheen, while in spring and summer the birds grow short crests. Cormorants are the larger of the two birds, but judging size at a distance is notoriously difficult, and several other points of difference are more readily observed. Adult cormorants have white face-patches and some have white heads and necks, although this is not normal in British or Norwegian birds. In the breeding season they develop white patches on the thighs. Their beaks are proportionately larger than those of shag. Young cormorants have entirely whitish underparts but young shags have no more than a whitish breast. Both species swim with beaks tilted upwards and fly with necks stretched out straight. When other features are not visible this helps to distinguish them from divers, which swim with beak almost horizontal and fly with the head held slightly below the line of the body.

Feeding on fish, both cormorants and shags have wettable plumage as this reduces their buoyancy and makes diving easier. Afterwards they can be seen standing holding their wings open to dry them out. Shags are strictly maritime, occurring along much of the Atlantic and Mediterranean coasts and nesting among rocks or in sea-caves. Cormorants are also found in the Baltic and may occur inland, notably in southeast Europe. They generally nest in more open situations and in more compact colonies than shags, on ledges and the tops of rock stacks; inland they will also use trees. Where both species occur together there is little competition for food as cormorants fish near the bottom, catching many flatfish, and shag hunt the middle waters taking fish such as sand-eels.

Grey Heron *Ardea cinerea* L 90cm

Grey herons are unlikely to be confused with other birds except possibly purple herons *(Ardea purpurea)* which are smaller, much darker and occur mostly as summer visitors to southern Europe. Juvenile grey herons are paler than adults and lack the black head plumes of breeding individuals. Herons stalk their prey in water and on land with a stealthy gait and long, frozen pauses. At rest they often hunch up their necks and stand on one leg. In flight the legs trail, the slow-beating wings are deeply bowed and the neck is withdrawn, unlike the much rarer cranes and storks which fly with necks outstretched. Largely associated with freshwater habitats, herons nest colonially in trees and, occasionally, in reed beds or on cliffs. They are resident throughout northwest Europe, but in most of Norway and Sweden occur only in summer. The total population fluctuates in relation to winter weather, since frozen conditions make feeding and survival difficult.

Bittern *Botaurus stellaris* L 76cm

A secretive brown bird, the bittern is far more often heard than seen. Fortunately its booming song is unique, resembling a distant foghorn, and may be heard from January to June. The rare view will usually be of a hunched-up bird which only reveals its long neck when catching prey or in its alarm posture – stretched up straight from feet to beak tip so that its striped brown plumage resembles the reed beds it inhabits. The flight is typically heron-like with rounded, down-curved wings and trailing green legs. Bitterns feed on a wide variety of creatures, mostly fish and amphibians but also smaller birds and mammals. They are resident over most of western Europe, but north of the Baltic occur only as summer visitors to southern Sweden. They are very rare in Britain due to the destruction of the large, undisturbed freshwater reed beds they require.

Great-crested Grebe *Podiceps cristatus* L 48cm

Their chestnut and black head tufts make great-crested grebes unmistakable in spring and summer but these are lost in winter, when the birds are grey above, with a white face, throat and underparts. Often they pull their heads down and thus look short-necked, but at other times they have a slim, upright appearance. They fly with trailing legs and outstretched heads, each wing showing two large white patches. The chicks are striped and often carried on the adults' backs for protection from pike and other predators. Found mainly on lowland fresh waters, great-crested grebes never come ashore except to clamber on to their floating nests, which they construct of reeds and other emergent plants, anchored amid the stems of water weeds or other vegetation. Their range extends throughout most of Europe except northern Scotland and much of Scandinavia. In winter large congregations may occur and some birds move to coastal waters.

Little Grebe *Tachybaptus ruficollis* L 27cm

Small, plump diving birds, in summer little grebes are dark brown with bright chestnut cheeks and throat, which contrast with a conspicuous greenish-yellow mark on the base of the beak. In the breeding season they are notably self-effacing and often it is only their strange whinnying call that betrays them. During winter they are less secretive, and tend to concentrate where feeding is good; at this time they are dark brown above and fawn below. Little grebes favour slow-flowing waters and ponds with well-vegetated margins, feeding on small fish, insect larvae and other animal life. Like the great-crested grebe, they build floating nests anchored amid water weeds, and normally the incubating bird covers the eggs before leaving, so that the nest looks like a patch of plant debris. Largely resident throughout western Europe, little grebes occur only as summer visitors in southern Sweden and are altogether absent from Norway.

Moorhen *Gallinula chloropus* L 33cm

Adult moorhens appear black with a white line along each flank, and an area of white under the tail. There is a red shield on the forehead that extends down the beak to meet the yellow tip. The commonest call is a rather harsh 'kurruk'. Young birds are brown and lack the red forehead. In the water, moorhens often swim with the 'stern' much higher than the chest and progress is jerky, with the head bobbing and tail flicking. On land, they reveal longish green legs and feet with very long toes which give them the ability to swim, to dive and to run, as well as providing support on floating vegetation. Found on almost all water bodies with vegetated margins (but keeping to the fringes of larger lakes) moorhens are very widespread, and are resident over western Europe except central Scandinavia where they are summer visitors.

Coot *Fulica atra* L 38cm

Coot are easily identifiable waterfowl, black all over with conspicuous white foreheads and beaks. Compared with moorhens, they appear rounder, and also spend more time afloat. Their legs are set further back and the toes have wide lobes — both adaptations giving better performance in water with a corresponding sacrifice of agility on land. Young coots are grey-brown above and pale whitish on throat and underparts. Coots have to run hard across the water, flapping at the same time, before they can take off and, like moorhens, they fly with legs trailing. Expert divers, they eat underwater plants and small animals. They also come ashore to graze, dashing back to the water at any sign of danger. In the breeding season, coots aggressively defend their territories, but in winter they may be found in large flocks. They have a similar range to moorhens but are more associated with bodies of open water.

Tufted Duck *Aythya fuligula* L 43cm

The male tufted duck is a distinctive metallic black with contrasting white flanks. The female is brown, and both sexes have small drooping crests, and in flight show broad, white trailing edges on the wings. Like other diving ducks they are compact, buoyant-looking birds and they share with their relatives the habit of rolling on their sides in the water when preening, to reveal paler underparts. Confusion with scaup *(Aythya marila)* is possible but scaup lack crests, the male scaup has a pale grey back, and the female scaup has a much larger white patch at the base of the beak than will be seen on any female tufted duck. Tufted ducks favour lakes, reservoirs and slow-moving rivers, feeding mainly on molluscs. They are resident in the British Isles, the Low Countries and the west Baltic. Scandinavian birds move south in winter, when tufted ducks also occur throughout southern Europe.

Pochard *Aythya ferina* L 46cm

The chestnut head, and the grey body with a black chest and tail, give the male pochard a typical diving duck plumage pattern which is simple and easy to recognize. The females are a much duller version of the male, with brown head and breast, and drab greyish body; despite this undistinguished appearance, identification is easy once one is familiar with them. In flight, both sexes show a dark head, neck and tail contrasting with a much paler body and wings. Pochard favour lowland freshwater sites where they largely feed on submerged aquatic plants. As breeding species, they are widely but rather thinly distributed in the British Isles, also occurring as residents over much of France, northeast to the Baltic and as summer visitors to Sweden. In winter there is a southward movement and a dispersal to larger waters, including reservoirs and gravel pits, where they often occur in mixed flocks with other diving ducks.

Goldeneye *Bucephala clangula* L 46cm

The white cheek patch that contrasts with the dark head makes an adult male goldeneye unlike any other duck. Females and young are basically grey with brown heads, but can look uniformly dark. However, they normally show a white mark (the speculum) on the edge of the folded wing, and goldeneyes of any age or sex have characteristically triangular heads with rather short beaks. In flight they look very black and white, with large white patches on the inner wing, and their rapid wing-beats produce a loud whistling. Goldeneyes feed on bottom-living animals, and the high-domed head has air-containing sinuses which may help in making long dives. Breeding mainly in Norway, Sweden and around the southern Baltic, goldeneyes nest in tree-holes, usually in conifer woods close to water. In winter they may be found throughout northeast Europe, often concentrated in large numbers on fresh or salt waters where food is plentiful.

Eider *Somateria mollissima* L 58cm

Eiders are seaducks, and even at long range the male's white above and black below pattern is easy to recognize, while in flight – usually low over the waves – they look white in front and black behind. The females are dark brown. Immatures and males in summer moult (eclipse plumage) present a variably black-and-white appearance but usually show a long white stripe on the flank. Feeding largely on mussels, eiders have strong beaks that slope up straight to the forehead, producing a most distinctive head shape. Often nesting in the open, eiders rely for protection on the cryptic plumage of the female, which will sometimes even build among a colony of gulls, benefiting from the 'air cover' they provide against other predators. Although many birds are resident around the coast of Scandinavia, Holland and the northern British Isles, others move south in winter and may be seen in the Mediterranean.

Wigeon *Anas penelope* L 46cm

The cream-and-chestnut head and pink chest of the male wigeon are unmistakable, as is the lovely whistling call, a high-pitched 'whee-oo'. In the air, drakes reveal large white rectangles on the forewing and even a few males in a distant flight will instantly identify it. The female is a noticeably rich brown, with a white belly – little like the overall grey-brown of duck mallard, pintail or teal. Both sexes have noticeably short beaks adapted for grazing; the wigeon is the only European duck which has adopted the mode of feeding which all the geese employ, and this habit is of course a valuable identification guide. Breeding mainly on moors and tundra in Britain, Norway, Sweden and northern Germany, wigeon move south and west in winter to open waters, marshes and estuaries where suitable grasses or intertidal plants provide abundant food.

Teal *Anas crecca* L 35cm

The drake teal's chestnut and green head is diagnostic, but at long range the white stripe along the body and the yellow rear are easier to see. Their very small size and the green speculum both help with identification, especially in the case of the brown females. Small size also emphasizes their fast flight, which tends to be erratic, with small parties wheeling and swerving in tight formation. The male's call is a distinctive musical 'crrit', not very loud but carrying far. The only species of comparable size is the garganey *(Anas querquedula)*; the female garganey is much like the female teal, but the male garganey has a brown head with a white eyestripe. Garganey are summer visitors to Europe whereas teal are generally resident, occurring as a breeding migrant only in Scandinavia. At all seasons, teal prefer waters with ample marginal vegetation and feed on small items, especially seeds, picked from the water surface.

Mallard *Anas platyrhynchos* L 58cm

The male mallard's dark green head and neck, narrow white collar and brown chest distinguish it from all other species. In summer, males moult into a temporary eclipse plumage of mottled brown, and can be distinguished from females only by their yellow, not brownish, beaks. The females have noticeably dark crowns and this helps to separate them from the smaller, slimmer female pintail and wigeon. Mallard are dabbling ducks, taking seeds and small creatures from the surface of the water, and feeding as far down as they can reach by upending. All this group of birds have a brightly coloured patch of feathers on the hindwing — the speculum — and only in the mallard is this dark blue. Mallard are the commonest European ducks, favouring shallow fresh waters but, for safety, often passing the day out on deeper waters, including estuaries. They are resident everywhere except in northern Scandinavia, where they are summer visitors.

Shoveler *Anas clypeata* L 50cm

For most of the year the male shoveler has a green head, white breast, and chestnut flanks and belly, but for a period in late summer the males — like other dabbling ducks — don eclipse plumage and are speckled brown, much like the females. Both sexes are identifiable by the pale blue forewing — visible in flight — and the huge, spatulate beak which gives them a flat-headed appearance and can usually be seen at long range. This beak contains a filtering mechanism, and the bird feeds by skimming it across the surface of the water or fluid mud, and sieving out small creatures and seeds. Because of the feeding method, shoveler favour the shallow, food-rich waters and marshes which occur in the lowlands; in winter they also use more open waters. Shoveler breed in the British Isles, France, the Low Countries and around the Baltic. There is a southerly movement in winter.

Pintail *Anas acuta* L male 66cm; female 56cm

The male pintail's brown head, contrasting white neck stripe and white throat are its best identification features. Actually smaller and slighter than the mallard, the male's greater length is due to its strikingly long tail feathers, which usually show up clearly when in flight, but may be less evident at long range on water. The mottled brown female's tail is shorter, and her rather slim appearance and brown head help to identify her; the heavier female mallard has a dark crown. In eclipse plumage the male becomes like the female but retains his dark head pattern. The male pintail's neck is longer than the female's and enables him to feed in deeper water, thus reducing competition between the sexes for food. They breed in marsh and moorland where shallow waters exist, sparsely in England and Scotland and northwest from Belgium. In winter they move southwest and occur throughout most of western Europe.

Red-breasted Merganser *Mergus serrator* L 58cm

Both sexes have a slender, 'efficient' look, being streamlined fish hunters. The long beak is equipped with serrated edges and a hooked tip for gripping slippery muscular prey. The drake's plumage is not unlike that of goosanders or even mallard, but note the brown chest, wide white collar and conspicuous crest. Females and immatures have a brown head and crest, pale throat and grey body, very similar to female and immature goosanders, but with a less sharply defined division between brown head and pale chest. Breeding on fresh water — usually in upland situations but also at coastal sites — the red-breasted merganser nests in dense cover on the ground. The range extends from southwest Ireland in a band running roughly northeast through Scotland, Denmark, north Germany and Scandinavia. Many birds move away from the breeding range to winter on estuaries and the sea all round Europe

Goosander *Mergus merganser* L 66cm

Goosanders are large, long-bodied ducks, the males exceptionally handsome with dark green heads, white chests and underparts often suffused with pink, and contrasting black backs. In flight they reveal a white inner wing, as do mergansers, but have more white on the body and back. Female goosanders are very similar to female mergansers but with a less projecting crest and a crisp divide between the brown head and the body. Goosanders are much less associated with salt water than mergansers, favouring clear, fast-flowing rivers in summer. Nesting for preference in tree holes, like other wildfowl, the female leads the young to water as soon as they hatch; they are so light that even a considerable .drop from the tree to the ground does them no harm. Breeding in northern Britain, Norway, Sweden and north Germany as well as central Europe, many goosanders move south in winter and are found over most of northern Europe, particularly on large lakes and reservoirs.

Shelduck *Tadorna tadorna* L 61cm

These unmistakable birds fall in a 'halfway house' between ducks and geese. The sexes are similar, except for a red knob on the male's beak. Their legs are set further forward than in most ducks and they are capable walkers. Unlike other ducks, both sexes go into eclipse plumage — a pale version of their normal pattern. Found in coastal situations, especially estuaries, shelducks feed on *Hydrobia*, a small and very numerous snail which lives in the intertidal zone. They nest in holes, especially rabbit burrows, and the young birds are gathered into large 'crèches' under the care of a few adults. After breeding the adults moult and become temporarily flightless, but first most congregate in moulting grounds which offer safety and assured food supplies. The largest of these is at the mouth of the river Elbe, Germany. Breeding round the coasts of northwest Europe, birds from the more northerly areas move south in winter.

Brent Goose *Branta bernicla* L 56–60cm

This is a very small goose – no bigger than the shelducks which share its estuarine wintering grounds. There are two races; the pale-bellied form breeds in Greenland and Spitzbergen and winters in flocks around northern Britain and Ireland. The dark-bellied race, an almost black goose, breeds in arctic Russia and winters from Denmark to Spain and around southern England. Size, colour and habitat together make confusion with other birds unlikely. Their primary winter food is an intertidal plant, eel grass, but recently some dark-bellied brent geese have started feeding on farmland because a great increase in their numbers has outstripped the natural food supply. This may be a temporary phase as the populations of these birds fluctuate greatly, as do those of other high-arctic breeding birds which may produce almost no young at all, sometimes for several years in succession, if the weather is unsuitable at the crucial time.

Greylag Goose *Anser anser* L 76–90cm

Several distinct grey geese occur in northwest Europe. Greylag geese are the only species present in summer outside northern Scandinavia and are the ancestors of farmyard geese, with similar calls. Until familiar with their finer points, beak colour is the best means of distinguishing different species. Greylag geese have large yellow beaks. White-fronted geese *(A. albifrons)* have white bands round the base of their beaks and irregular black barring on the belly. Pink-footed geese *(A. brachyrhynchus)* have smallish black-and-pink beaks, while those of bean geese *(A. fabalis)* are orange and black. The sexes are similar. Geese usually fly in diagonal lines or two diagonals forming a V, each bird setting up air currents which help the following one to fly with less effort. Greylag geese breed in Britain, Scandinavia and eastern Europe, with southerly winter movements. The other species are northern breeders wintering in flocks in mild areas, notably the coastal zone rather than the colder central European regions.

Canada Goose *Branta canadensis* L 92–102cm

Both sexes of this goose have black heads and necks with a white face patch. Their bodies are brown and they have the white rumps and dark-tipped tails also common to all European geese. Canada geese, like other geese, are primarily adapted to grazing and they may feed far from water on agricultural land, but they roost afloat for safety. They also nest close to water, building on the ground – often on islands. Both adults help to defend the nest and young, unlike ducks where the female depends largely on camouflage and the male plays no part in rearing the young. First introduced to Britain more than 250 years ago, Canada geese are now fairly widespread and locally numerous as a resident breeding species. They are also established in southern Scandinavia, and wintering birds are sometimes seen as far south as central Europe.

Mute swan *Cygnus olor* L 150cm

The orange-and-black beaks of mute swans help to distinguish them from two much rarer swans — whooper *(C. cygnus)* and Bewick's *(C. columbianus)* — both of which have yellow and black beaks. Whooper swans are the same size as mute swans but tend to hold their necks straighter. Bewick's are smaller and have shorter necks, rather like large geese. Immature mute swans are grey-brown with dull pink beaks, progressively gaining adult colours as they mature. Mute swans are largely silent birds, but in flight their primary feathers produce a rich throbbing which is quite unmistakable. Whooper and Bewick's swans call frequently when flying. Found largely on inland waters, but in winter also on estuaries, the mute swan is resident in the British Isles and from central France east to the Baltic, occurring in southern Sweden mainly as a summer visitor. Bewick's and whooper swans are both winter visitors to parts of northwest Europe from more northerly breeding grounds.

White Stork *Ciconia ciconia* L 102cm

On the ground, a white stork is not likely to be confused with any other species, with its large white body and black-ended wings, red legs and beak. In flight storks extend their necks, unlike herons which retract them. However, increasing numbers of escaped flamingos now occur in northwest Europe and these may have a similar appearance in flight if they have lost most of their pink colouring, although their legs project very far beyond the tail, and their beaks are heavy and down-curved. White storks feed on insects, small mammals and reptiles in marshy areas and grasslands. In northwestern Europe, nearly all individuals construct their large nests on the roofs or chimneys of buildings. Their numbers have greatly declined and they are now very rare in many places where, until recently, they were well known and affectionately regarded. They occur as summer visitors to Spain and very sparsely north to Denmark.

Gannet *Sula bassana* L 90cm

Gannets are massive seabirds with a 1.80m wingspan. Adults are white with black tips to their wings and yellow-tinted heads. At a distance they look pure white, unlike gulls which look greyish or dark. Immature birds are dark brown, gradually becoming whiter as they mature. Gannets feed on fish which they catch by diving headfirst from altitudes up to 30m or more, folding back their wings to resemble paper darts as they enter the water. Their eyes are set well forward in the head to give the binocular vision necessary for judging the speed and distance of prey, and the skull is specially adapted to absorb the dive impact. Nesting colonially, the main breeding population is in Britain and Ireland where a total of sixteen sites holds over 140,000 out of the world population of about 200,000 birds. Other colonies are in Iceland, Norway and Brittany.

Great Black-backed Gull *Larus marinus* L 65–80cm [illustrated] / **Lesser
Black-backed Gull** *Larus fuscus* L 53–56cm

Great black-backed gulls are the size of small geese; in flight they have black
backs, and wings with a narrow white margin. Wing-beats are slow and deep,
but progress is rapid. At close range the massive beak and pink legs are
visible. Scandinavian lesser black-backed gulls are similarly dark, but the
British race has a light grey back. The head and beak are less bulky and the legs
are bright yellow. Calls also differ, great black-backed gulls having a deep
barking 'owk, owk' while lesser black-backed gulls' calls are higher pitched
and more quickly uttered – like those of herring gulls. Immatures of both
species are heavily mottled with brown, gaining adult colour as they mature.
Both species are scavengers and predators. They breed in coastal situations on
open ground in Brittany, the British Isles, Scandinavia and the Baltic. Lesser
black-backed gulls in particular are migrants over most of their range and may
occur well inland in winter.

Herring Gull *Larus argentatus* L 56–66cm

Herring gulls have grey mantles, and wings with black tips marked by white
spots. Like other large gulls their beaks are yellow with a red mark; the legs of
those seen in western Europe are pink. Elsewhere there is some similarity in
mantle and leg colour with lesser black-backed gulls but here the only danger
of confusion is with the smaller common gull. Separation of brown, immature
herring gulls and lesser black-backed gulls is difficult. Herring gulls nest on the
grassy tops of cliffs, on offshore islands, coastal dunes and, locally, on the
roofs of buildings. Each pair defends a small territory within the colony.
Although unguarded eggs or young are eaten by neighbours there are overall
advantages in colonial breeding, including excellent mass defence against
more dangerous predators. Herring gulls are found almost all round Europe's
coast throughout the year, with some summer migration in Scandinavia, and in
winter they spread widely inland.

Common Gull *Larus canus* L 41cm

Common gulls are smaller than herring gulls, but this is often difficult to judge.
Flight is rather more graceful; also head and beak appear relatively smaller in
relation to overall size than in herring gulls. Definite identification points are
that the beak is yellow-green, lacking any red spot, and that the legs are also
greenish. Like other gulls, this species takes a wide variety of food – mostly
invertebrates such as worms and insects but also fish, small mammals, eggs
and chicks. Throughout their breeding range they are found inland as well as
on the coasts, mostly nesting close to water but also on open moorland. They
are often, but not invariably, colonial. Present all year round on northern
European coasts, they occur as summer migrants inland in Scandinavia. In
autumn many move south, reaching the Mediterranean; fewer winter inland
than is the case with herring gulls.

Black-headed Gull *Larus ridibundus* L 36cm

Black-headed gulls are one of the easiest species to identify. In summer they have chocolate hoods, and these are lost in autumn when the birds have white heads with dark ear-like marks behind each eye. At all seasons they have red legs and beaks. In flight the grey back and inner wing contrast with a wedge of white feathers running down the forewing to the tip, the trailing edge of which has a black border. Young birds have much brown in the plumage, dark tail tips and paler beaks and legs. Like most other gulls, black-headed gulls have become much more numerous in the last century, and feed on a wide variety of animal matter in all sorts of situations including farmland and rubbish tips. They breed by water over most of northern Europe except northern Scandinavia, and in winter they also occur around the Mediterranean.

Kittiwake *Rissa tridactyla* L 41cm

A wholly marine gull, the kittiwake shows adaptation to life out at sea with slender wings and a very buoyant flight. It is the only common species with all-black triangular tips to the pale grey wings. On the ground it is also possible to see the yellow beak and short black legs. The 'kittee-wayk' call is heard mostly at nesting colonies. Immatures have a broad dark line forming a characteristic W across the wings and back; the tail has a black tip. Kittiwakes feed on small marine animals picked from the surface of the sea and rarely stray inland, unlike other gulls. Breeding in France, the British Isles, Denmark and Norway, they build on cliff ledges in clamorous colonies, each nest just out of pecking distance of its neighbour. In winter the birds disperse widely over the Atlantic and into the western Mediterranean.

Fulmar *Fulmarus glacialis* L 47cm

Although gull-like at first glance, the fulmar is readily distinguished from true gulls by a lack of any black markings, and also by its flight. The wings are held straight and stiff for long periods as the bird rides air currents, gliding smoothly and fast across the cliff face or low over the sea. This special skill enables fulmars, and related species including the albatrosses, to travel far at sea with little expenditure of energy. Even in flapping flight, the wings remain stiff. It is thought that the availability of offal from fishing fleets is at least partly responsible for the remarkable expansion of the fulmar's range that has occurred since the late nineteenth century. Fulmars have spread from Iceland and St Kilda to colonize almost all the suitable coastal sites – mostly cliffs – around Ireland and Britain, and reached Norway and Britanny. The birds wander widely at sea, feeding on floating animal matter, live or dead.

Common Tern *Sterna hirundo* L 35cm [illustrated]/**Arctic Tern**
Sterna paradisea L 35cm

Terns are easily distinguished by their slender build, long, narrow wings
without black tips, and forked tails. They often hover before diving headfirst
into water to catch small fish. Their calls are usually high-pitched and harsh,
typically 'keeyah'. Common terns and arctic terns are rather alike; both have
red beaks, but the common tern's beak has a black tip, and it is often difficult to
separate them in flight. Juveniles have white foreheads and dark beaks. Do
not confuse these species with the bigger Sandwich tern (*Sterna sandvicensis*,
L 41cm) with its yellow-tipped black beak, or with the very small little tern
(*Sterna albifrons*, L 24cm) with a black-tipped, yellow beak and a white
forehead. All are summer visitors to Europe, nesting mainly on shingle and
sandy beaches on undisturbed coasts. Common terns breed in western
European countries and often nest inland. Arctic terns nest from France
northward; Sandwich and little terns, less numerously, from the Baltic south.

Black Tern *Chlidonias niger* L 24cm

Three species of marsh tern occur in Europe, the black tern being the most
widespread. Its upperparts are dark grey, with lighter grey underwings and
tail, and sooty black chest and head. Although this sounds rather depressing
plumage, they are in fact most attractive birds. They are dainty in the air with
rapid light wing beats, dropping frequently to the water's surface to take
insects which they also catch in flight, but rarely diving into the water.
Juveniles and winter adults are white below with a dark mark in front of each
wing. Black terns usually build floating nests anchored by water plants,
breeding colonially in marshes and around reed-fringed lakes and rivers.
Nesting is often sporadic, and the drainage of suitable shallow wetlands
continues to fragment their range. They are summer visitors to Europe north to
Denmark, but only occur on migration in Britain.

Ringed Plover *Charadrius hiaticula* L 19cm [illustrated]/**Little Ringed
Plover** *Charadrius dubius* L 15cm

In summer, adult ringed plovers and little ringed plovers have rather similar
head patterns, but the former has an orange-and-black beak and orange legs
while the latter's beak is dark, and its legs are dull pink or yellowish. In flight,
ringed plovers show a white wing bar, but little ringed plovers do not.
Juveniles are paler than the adults, which themselves tend to be less strongly
marked in winter. Little ringed plovers are summer visitors to Europe; their
natural habitat is sand or pebble banks on rivers, but they have greatly
expanded their range by using gravel workings. They reached Britain in the
mid-1940s and now occur over most of England, and in Sweden and Norway.
Ringed plovers are birds of beaches, although a few breed inland on sandy
heaths and gravel pits. They are resident in Britain, occurring as summer
migrants further north — these birds winter on the Atlantic and Mediterranean
coasts.

Dunlin *Calidris alpina* L 17–19cm

Dunlins are rather dumpy birds with shortish legs and beaks that are slightly down-curved towards the tip. In winter the plumage is grey-brown above and pale below, with birds progressively developing rich brown backs and black bellies as the breeding season approaches. Many variations between the two extremes may be seen in autumn when moulting adults and juveniles appear. In flight, dunlins have a narrow white wing bar, and the tail is black with a small white patch on each side. Outside the breeding season, dunlins are the commonest shore bird, occurring in flocks that may be several thousand strong on the estuaries of western Europe, where they run busily over the mudflats, probing for food; they also occur around inland waters. Dunlin breed on tundra in Scandinavia, on coastal salt marshes and river valleys around the Baltic, and on moorland and northern marshes in the British Isles.

Common Sandpiper *Tringa hypoleucos* L 20cm

The common sandpiper is a small, brown-backed wader with dark sides to the breast almost forming a bib, white underparts and a most characteristic habit of constantly bobbing its tail. In flight it shows a white wing bar and white sides to the tail, rather like a dunlin, but with a distinctive flicking wing action and a ringing 'twee-wee-wee' call. Common sandpipers breed by fresh water; in the British Isles largely on upland rivers and lakes but elsewhere also in lowland situations and among woodland. They are widespread summer visitors to suitable habitats in almost all of Europe. Most birds winter in Africa; some remain in a coastal, and hence mild, belt running from France and Iberia right round the northern Mediterranean, and others winter even further north. Like many waders, they may be seen briefly in many sorts of wetland situation when on passage.

Green Sandpiper *Tringa ochropus* L 23cm [illustrated] / **Wood Sandpiper** *Tringa glareola* L 20cm

A medium-sized wader with dark grey-brown upperparts, a lighter brown breast and white underparts. Both beak and legs are longer than those of the smaller and paler common sandpiper. Green sandpipers appear very black and white, especially in flight when the dark back and wings contrast strongly with the white rump and underparts. The rather similar wood sandpiper is browner with lighter underwings and legs that project further beyond the tail in flight. Both species are very nervous, often flushing at some distance. The green sandpiper has a ringing triple-note call; the wood sandpiper's is weaker. In the breeding season, both species are distributed eastward from Norway, Sweden and eastern Germany in old, swampy conifer forests and wet alder woods. During autumn green sandpipers move south and west to winter largely on inland fresh waters in a belt extending southeast from southern Ireland and Britain; wood sandpipers leave Europe altogether.

Grey Plover *Pluvialis squatarola* L 28cm

Although the grey plover breeds in northern Russia, birds may be seen in Europe in summer plumage just before migrating north. Then they have black faces and underparts, contrasting with mottled grey backs; the two separated by a broad white band. Most sightings will, however, be of birds in winter, when they are rather light grey overall except for a white eyestripe and belly. In flight, at all seasons they reveal white rumps and barred tails, as well as black patches in the 'armpits' of otherwise white underwings – all points serving to separate them from golden plovers. The main wintering habitat is coastal mudflats round most of western Europe, south from Scotland and north Germany. All plovers share a distinctive feeding method – they stand still and look, then run a few paces and grab the prey. This helps to distinguish them from similar shore birds, which busily probe at random.

Golden Plover *Pluvialis apricaria* L 28cm

In winter, the golden plover appears as a browner version of the grey plover, distinguishable in flight by the uniformly dark rump and tail and by the lack of a black 'armpit'. Summer plumage varies; birds breeding in the far north have black underparts, throats and faces but further south this colouring extends less far up the chest. The upperparts are spangled with gold. Golden plovers nest on moors and tundra mainly in Scandinavia, northern Britain and Ireland where their call – a liquid and melancholy whistle – 'tlui' – often draws attention to the bird standing watching you. As with many other waders, an approach to the nest or young by a predator produces a distraction display, the adult feigning injury and tumbling over the ground just out of reach until it has drawn the danger off. Golden plovers winter south to the Mediterranean on food-rich grasslands, often in large flocks and in company with lapwings.

Knot *Calidris canutus* L 25cm

In summer plumage the knot is a distinctive and handsome bird with rich rufous back and deep reddish breast and belly. Unfortunately they are rarely seen in Europe in full breeding dress, and during the winter they are both duller and harder to identify, having pale grey backs and white underparts. In flight the wings are pale beneath and the faint white wing bar is often hardly noticeable. Indeed, the absence of contrasting features like the grey plover's black 'armpit', or the brown and white pattern of the redshank, is a good pointer to the knot's identity. Breeding outside Europe on Arctic tundra, knot winter on the coasts from Denmark and the British Isles, south into the Mediterranean. They are largely confined to estuarine habitats, where they feed on small molluscs in the intertidal mud. Both when feeding and at roost above the high tide, knot typically form large, closely packed flocks.

Snipe *Gallinago gallinago* L 37cm

The remarkably long, straight beak of the snipe is the obvious identification feature of this wader. Snipe feed in marshy ground and pools, probing deep for worms and insect grubs. Their cryptic markings make them hard to see and often they are flushed unexpectedly, when they rise fast with a zig-zag flight and a rasping 'schape' call. In the breeding season males perform extensive circular display flights during which they alternately rise and dive obliquely; as they descend a specially shaped feather on each side of the tail is projected at right angles, vibrating in its passage through the air to produce a protracted, bleating note. Snipe also have a song, often uttered from a fence post – a repeated and rather clock-like 'chip-per'. Generally resident in northwest Europe, snipe occur only during summer in most of Norway and Sweden and are largely winter visitors to the Mediterranean countries.

Ruff *Philomachus pugnax* L male 29cm; female 23cm

In the breeding season, males wear a remarkable ruff and ear tufts in greatly variable combinations of black, white and brown, and display on open grassy sites called leks, where the mottled brown females (called reeves) come to be mated by the dominant males. At other seasons males resemble females although they are appreciably larger, on the ground appearing much like redshank but with noticeably shorter beaks – an important and reliable identification feature. Beak and leg colour are very variable, frequently yellow or green; the legs are never red. In flight they show very little white, having only a narrow white wing bar and striking oval white patches on each side of the dark tail. Ruffs breed in wet grassland and marshes in Europe east and north from Holland and (very sparsely) in England. Most birds move in winter at least as far as the coasts of southwest and southern Europe.

Redshank *Tringa totanus* L 28cm

A common wader, the redshank is easily recognized by its long orange-red legs and beak. In flight it has a broad white hindwing with a white rump and lightly barred white tail, which form an obvious identification feature. Redshanks are conspicuous and noisy birds; the call is a loud piping 'tee-tu-tu', and both hysterical alarm and trilling song are variations on this theme. Nesting in wet meadows and salt marshes, redshanks are fairly widespread in their breeding range but like snipe and other waders that breed in western Europe they are declining greatly due to land drainage improvement. They are distributed in a broad coastal belt around Europe and throughout the British Isles, being resident in many areas but occurring only as a summer visitor to eastern Europe and most of Scandinavia. In winter, most birds move to estuaries and, like many other waders, may occur in large flocks.

Curlew *Numenius arquata* L 53–58cm

Usually the very long (up to 15cm) down-curved beak, looking almost too large to support, is easy to see. Curlew, have a rather leisurely but purposeful flight, revealing white rumps, and often seem to look more grey than brown. The commonest call is a ringing 'cour-lee' and on the breeding grounds the song, usually delivered in flight, is loud, slow and liquid and includes a beautiful bubbling trill. Confusion with a whimbrel *(Numenius phaeopus)* is possible as this, too, has a down-curved beak and white rump but it is only about two-thirds the size of a curlew, with a dark-striped crown, and a call consisting of an even succession of six or seven whistled notes. Nesting in damp country – moorland, wet grassland and heaths – curlews breed north from central France, most of the Scandinavian population being migratory. In winter birds occur on coastal marshes and other wetlands south to the Mediterranean.

Bar-tailed Godwit *Limosa lapponica* L 38cm

In most of Europe it is relatively uncommon to see bar-tailed godwits in summer plumage, when they are strikingly russet-red on the face, neck and underparts, the colour extending right under the belly to the tail and providing a point of distinction from the black-tailed godwit in which the undertail remains white. In winter, bar-tailed godwits become brown above and whitish below; like all such waders, transitional plumages may be seen in autumn and spring when the red is more or less mottled white. They are a little smaller in all respects than black-tailed godwits, and when they take flight the lack of a wing bar, the white lower back and rump, and lightly barred tail readily distinguish them. Bar-tailed godwits breed in the far north of Scandinavia and Russia on damp tundra, wintering on the estuaries of western Europe where they feed on invertebrates.

Black-tailed Godwit *Limosa limosa* L 41cm

In flight, black-tailed godwits display a conspicuous white wing bar, the tail is white on the basal half and black on the tip, and the legs project well beyond the end of the tail. On the ground matters are more complicated because the bar-tailed godwit is very similar in both brown winter and rufous summer plumage. However, when the two species are observed together, the black-tailed godwit can be seen to be distinctly longer legged and to have a slightly longer beak. In the breeding season, black-tailed godwits are found on damp grassland and wet heaths. At the start of this period, the males are very evident in their display flights and calling. Breeding only very locally and in small numbers in Britain, France and Sweden – but more numerously from Holland eastward through Denmark and Germany – they migrate to western European coasts in winter.

Turnstone   *Arenaria interpres*   L 23cm

Turnstones are strikingly patterned shore birds with a rather stout, short-legged appearance. During winter the rich chestnut-and-black feathering is replaced by a drabber grey-brown and they look more uniformly dark above and white below. Despite this, they appear unlike other waders, and in flight the bold pattern of white, black and brown makes turnstone identification simple. Their behaviour is also rather distinctive. They probe for food among weeds and small stones, often turning objects with their beaks, and they prefer weedy and rocky shores, where their coloration makes them surprisingly easy to overlook so that sometimes it is only the movement of their orange-red legs that gives them away. Breeding in Europe on or close to the coast of Scandinavia, turnstones move south in autumn, when they may occasionally be seen inland, to winter on milder shores, mostly around the North Sea and facing the Atlantic.

Oystercatcher   *Haematopus ostralegus*   L 43cm

The oystercatcher is black with white underparts, and has a stout orange beak and pink legs. In winter it has a white throat band. In flight the pied effect is very evident as a broad white wing bar, white rump and underwing are revealed. The powerful beak is used for opening cockles and mussels and in probing for worms. Individual birds tend to specialize on prey species and on the method of opening them — some birds smash through the shell; other skilfully nip through the muscle that holds it shut. At one season or another oystercatchers may be found anywhere on the European coasts, but basically there is a resident population in western Europe and on parts of the Mediterranean, and this is much supplemented in winter by birds which breed further north and right round Scandinavia. As well as nesting on the coast, oystercatchers also occur inland, for example in Scottish river valleys.

Avocet   *Recurvirostra avosetta*   L 43cm

Avocets are quite unlike other waders, with their black-on-white plumage and long recurved beaks. Flying at long range, when the beak cannot be seen, they are still unlike any other bird, with a black crown and V on the shoulders, a diagonal bar across each wing and black wing tips. In western Europe, they breed on brackish and salt coastal lagoons from Denmark, Holland and eastern England to the Mediterranean, and may be found wintering on estuaries south from southwest England. Their specialized beaks are used not for probing or picking like other waders, but for sweeping from side-to-side through water and liquid mud to capture small invertebrates, especially brine shrimps. In the northern part of their range suitable habitat is scarce and breeding success variable, as only optimum conditions produce the flush of food necessary for the survival of the young. Like many other waders, avocets can swim competently.

Lapwing *Vanellus vanellus* L 30cm

In flight, a lapwing looks black above with a white rump, and white below with black outer wings. The wings are rounded, and appear broader at the tips than at their junction with the body. Wing-beats are leisurely. Close up, the bird's iridescent green, chestnut and black markings and long up-curving crest can be distinguished. Resident throughout northwest Europe, but only summer visitors in mid-Scandinavia, lapwings inhabit open country, feeding mainly on insects and other small invertebrates picked up from the ground. They breed before the summer warmth has dried up the soil's surface and made food for the young hard to find. The adults defend the nest and young – driving away predators with vigorous dive-bombing and loud 'pee-wit' calls. In winter, lapwings often occur in large flocks especially on grassland; western and southern areas, particularly, receive massive sudden influxes as a response to cold snaps further north or east.

Red Grouse [illustrated]/**Willow Grouse** *Lagopus lagopus* L 38–41cm

These birds belong to the same species despite different plumages, which have resulted from their evolution in different areas with different conditions. Both are stout birds with broad, rounded wings. They normally fly very low, with bursts of whirring wing-beats interspersed by glides, and both species give the familiar 'go-back, go-back' call, sounding like a loud, mechanical voice. The red grouse is a rich, dark brown with white underwing markings. Willow grouse have all-white wings in summer, plus some white on the underparts and, in winter, turn white all over except for the black tail; at all seasons, they resemble ptarmigan *(Lagopus mutus)* which, however, live at higher altitudes. Red grouse are found only in the British Isles, and then only on moorland with heather, the shoots of which they eat. Willow grouse occur in northern Scandinavia on tundra with willow and birch scrub or heather.

Black Grouse *Lyrurus tetrix* L male 53cm; female 41cm

The male (blackcock) has a rich, blue-black plumage and a most unusual lyre-shaped tail. In flight it reveals white bars along the upper wing. The female (greyhen) resembles a red grouse but is greyer, has a slightly forked tail and, like the male, a largely white underwing. Males display communally at a breeding site called a lek, with wings drooped, tails spread and loud bubbling calls. The dominant individuals win central territories in the lek and it is they who mate with almost all of the females, which are then entirely responsible for nest-building, incubation and rearing the young. Black grouse favour moor and heathland associated with the edges of conifer and birch woods; young conifer plantations are very attractive and have aided their recent British expansion. They are resident in western and northern Britain and in Scandinavia, central and eastern Europe, but are absent from Ireland, Iberia, Italy and most of France.

Pheasant *Phasianus colchicus* L male 66–89cm; female 53–63cm

Pheasants are familiar birds which need little description. There is considerable variation in the markings and colour of males because several species of
pheasant have been released in Europe and interbred since the original intro-
duction of the Caucasian type, at an unrecorded but certainly very ancient date.
Thus many birds have white collars, some are pale fawn and others extremely
dark blue-green. The male's crow is a ringing 'kurr-kuk', repeated almost
hysterically as an alarm call. Generally, females are a uniform mottled brown.
In moult, they and the short-tailed juveniles can look superficially like partridges. Found throughout most of Europe except Portugal and northern
Scandinavia, pheasants roost in trees for safety, but feed on the ground on
young shoots of plants, berries, seeds and small animal life, using their strong
legs and feet to turn over the leaf litter and surface soil as they search for
them.

Grey Partridge *Perdix perdix* L 30cm

Partridges are plump, chicken-like birds. The male grey partridge is very
handsome, its orange face contrasting with the pale grey neck and breast, the
flanks delicately barred with chestnut and with a large brown horseshoe
mark on the belly. The female is paler, sometimes lacking the horseshoe altogether, as juveniles do. Grey partridges are often seen in large groups (coveys)
but are not conspicuous, and birds quietly feeding or dust-bathing are easily
overlooked. They fly more willingly than red-legged partridges, whirring
noisily and then gliding with down-curved wings to settle at a safe distance.
Their call is most often heard at dusk and dawn – a grating 'keev' or 'krr'ic'.
Found mainly on arable farmland, but increasingly rare in areas of intensive
modern agriculture, grey partridges are a widespread European resident,
absent only in the far south, notably most of Spain, and in the north of
Scandinavia.

Red-legged Partridge *Alectoris rufa* L 34cm

Male and female red-legged partridges are identical, with white faces strongly
marked by a black eyestripe and throat, and with heavily barred tails. Juveniles
are paler, unbarred versions of the adults. Like other gamebirds, red-legged
partridges are adapted to life on the ground, with an upright stance and strong
legs and feet. When disturbed they will run rapidly or vanish into cover and
only become airborne if danger approaches closely; then they fly low on
rounded brown wings and demonstrate another typical gamebird feature of
rapid flapping, interspersed by glides. Their call is a lound 'ch'kar, ch'kar'.
Their main natural range is Iberia and southern France, but red-legged
partridges were introduced into Britain in the eighteenth century, and in open
habitats in southeast England they are now often more numerous than the
grey partridge. A closely related species, the rock partridge *(Alectoris graeca)*
occurs elsewhere in southern Europe.

Wood Pigeon *Columba palumbus* L 41cm

Wood pigeons are very common birds in the countryside and even in some towns. They are generally wary and difficult to watch in woodland, but are frequently seen well in open farmland, and in flight. On the ground, the white neck-patch and white line along the edge of the wing easily distinguish the adults from other doves; in the air the white wing mark forms a conspicuous and diagnostic diagonal bar. Juveniles lack the neck patch, but have the wing bar. The flight is usually fast and direct, the wings often producing a loud clapping sound on take-off. Wood pigeons breed in woodland and have a five-syllable song 'coo-coo-coo, coo-coo', with a stress on the second note. They occur throughout Europe, except northern Scandinavia, and in winter many migrants move south and west from the most northerly and eastern parts of the range.

Stock Dove *Columba oenas* L 33cm

Smaller and generally less common than wood pigeons, stock doves have no white markings. On the ground they lack the heavy black wing bars of the rock dove; in flight, they have conspicuously dark wing tips and completely grey backs, whereas rock doves display white rumps. Young birds lack the iridescent sheen on the neck. The song is a repeated monotonous double 'coo'. Stock doves are hole-nesting birds and thus occur as a breeding species most commonly where old trees are plentiful, although they will also occasionally nest in rock cavities, holes in buildings and other similar situations. They feed largely on seeds and, like other doves, rear their young on a special secretion, 'pigeon's milk', which has a high protein content and is easily digested by the chicks. They occur throughout most of Europe except northern Scandinavia, but are resident only in western and southern areas.

Rock Dove or Feral Pigeon *Columba livia* L 33cm

The points which distinguish true rock doves from other pigeons are the double black wing bars, white rumps and white underwings. They are birds of rock and cliff faces both in mountainous country and on the coast, their range extending across southern Europe and up the western seaboard to the British Isles, where birds which probably have not interbred with the domestic strain are found in the Shetland Isles and western Ireland. Rock doves are the ancestors of domesticated pigeons which escaped to form the feral population found breeding in built-up areas and many cliff sites throughout Europe. These feral pigeons occur in many plumage variations and patterns, from brick-red through blue chequer to black or white. Individuals can often be seen with all the characteristics of the true rock dove. Like other pigeons, rock doves are mainly seed eaters, and both wild and feral forms may be found flocking in fields to feed.

Turtle Dove *Streptopelia turtur* L 27cm

Identification of turtle doves is quite simple once you can recognize the distinctive flight style shared with collared doves, and can see the points of difference between the two species. Turtle doves are small, slender pigeons and their most obvious identification features are their grey heads and the rich tortoiseshell patterning on the back. In flight, the underside of the rather long tail is black with a white end, unlike collared doves which appear to have more white than black on the tail. Both species may fly with the wings turned sharply back from the angle, and have a flicking flight action which is easily recognizable. Turtle doves prefer rather open wood and scrub country and are often seen when feeding on the ground. The song is a repeated soporific purring 'turr, turr'. The main breeding range reaches north as far as southern Britain and Denmark, and they leave Europe in winter.

Collared Dove *Streptopelia decaocto* L 32cm

Collared doves give an overall impression of being pale grey or cream-coloured, and adults are easily recognized by their black half-collars. In flight, the upper wingtips are dark and contrast with the lighter grey and brown of the rest of the upperparts. The underside of the tail is white with a black base Typically, collared doves and turtle doves fly fast, direct, and often low, with wingtips sharply angled back, using a flicking action. The song is a repeated 'coo-coo, coo' accented on the second syllable. This species has achieved a dramatic expansion of its range since the beginning of the century, steadily spreading across Europe from the extreme southeast to occur as a resident everywhere except in Italy, Iberia and northern Scandinavia. It is particularly associated with human settlements and large flocks occur where food is plentiful, such as around grain stores.

Little Owl *Athene noctua* L 22cm

The little owl is distinguished from other common northwest European owls by its small size and bounding, rather woodpecker-like flight, by the lack of ear tufts and by a rather frowning expression. It is a partly diurnal species and is most likely to be seen perched on a post or up close to the trunk of a tree. Feeding largely on the ground on worms, insects and other invertebrates, it is resident over Europe north to the Baltic, excluding Ireland and most of Scotland. In the southern half of its range, the similar-sized scops owl *(Otus scops)* occurs as a summer visitor and is distinguished by its ear tufts and less bounding flight. Over central Europe, Norway and Sweden, two other small species — Tengmalm's owl *(Aegolius funereus)* and the pygmy owl *(Glaucidium passerinum)* — occur, but they tend to be found mainly in conifer woodland rather than in the farmland and open woods preferred by little owls.

Barn Owl *Tyto alba* L 34cm

Barn owls will usually be seen at night. The most common view is of a pale, long-winged shape drifting silently along the roadside verge or perched upright, dark eyes staring from the flat facial disc. However, barn owls regularly hunt at dawn and dusk, and even in daylight when food is short or they are feeding young. The western race, found in Britain, is very pale, but those elsewhere in northern Europe are usually much darker coloured below. Barn owls prefer rather open country – such as farmland with few trees – rather than woodland which is the domain of the tawny owl. Their call is a strangled screech and they also make hissing and snoring noises at the daytime roost or nest-site which is often high up in a barn or little-used building. Barn owls are residents throughout western Europe north to the Baltic.

Short-eared Owl *Asio flammeus* L 38cm

This is the most likely owl to be seen in daylight. Short-eared owls are birds of open treeless country such as moorland, tundra and salt marsh. They usually fly fairly low when hunting, steadily quartering the ground. With their long wings, they glide and soar like harriers, but also exhibit a slow-looking flapping flight. The owl's enormous head and short tail prevent confusion with other birds of prey, and further identification is given by the dark patches at the bend on both upper and underwing surfaces. The ear tufts are rarely visible. Short-eared owl numbers fluctuate greatly, depending on the availability of their principal prey, rodents. Resident in north Britain and northeastward from the French coast through Denmark and Germany, short-eared owls are largely summer visitors to Norway and Sweden, with most birds moving south in autumn. During the winter they may be found throughout central and southern Europe.

Tawny Owl *Strix aluco* L 38cm

Tawny owls are essentially nocturnal birds of deciduous woodland, and are far more heard than seen. The best-known call is the familiar, quavering hoot, 'hoo-hoo-hoo, hooo'; they also produce a sharp 'ke-vick'. Very young birds utter a squeaky sound, like rusty hinges. During the day, tawny owls roost in thick cover such as ivy, and often the presence of a roosting owl is given away by small birds, which will persistently mob it. Surprisingly variable in colour from greyish to dark brown, tawny owls live mainly on small mammals, but also take sleeping birds. Because they inhabit woodland, where night hunting success depends on an intimate knowledge of the area, adult tawny owls are strictly resident and there is high mortality among young birds before they find vacant territories and learn to hunt in them. Their range covers most of Europe, excluding Ireland and northern Norway and Sweden.

Marsh Harrier *Circus aeruginosus* L 48–56cm

All harriers are low-altitude hunters with a slow, investigative flight, typically gliding with wingtips held higher than the body, in a shallow V. They also have acute hearing and thus can seek prey even in fairly dense cover. The male marsh harrier has blue-grey outer wings and tail, with brown inner wings and body. The head is pale. Females and immatures are dark brown above and below, with creamy heads and a pale leading edge to the inner wing. Feeding on small to medium-sized animals, such as coots, water voles and frogs, marsh harriers hunt in wet, marshy habitats and breed primarily in reed beds, nesting on the ground. Some males are polygamous. Now extremely rare in Britain, marsh harriers are widespread in Europe as far north as Sweden and Finland, although absent from Norway. In most northerly countries they occur only as summer visitors.

Montagu's Harrier *Circus pygarus* L 41–46cm [illustrated]/**Hen Harrier** *Circus cyaneus* L 43–51cm

Both male Montagu's harriers and male hen harriers are pale grey birds with black wingtips. They are distinguished mainly by the black line along the hind-wing of Montagu's harrier and by the hen harrier's white rump. Females of the two species are both brown with white rumps and barred tails, and although Montagu's harriers have more slender wings, this is not easy to spot. Young birds resemble the female, and most bird-watchers usually evade the issue and identify them all simply as 'ringtails'. Both species breed on heath, moorland, in young conifer plantations and in marshes where prey such as reptiles, birds and rodents are plentiful. Hen harriers are more associated with uplands in summer, although they often winter in lowland situations such as coastal marshes, when birds that breed in northern Scandinavia migrate south. Montagu's harriers occur in Europe only as a summer visitor and are absent from Norway, and almost all Sweden and Great Britain.

Osprey *Pandion haliaetus* L 51–58cm

The osprey's dark brown upperparts contrasting with the lightly marked white plumage below, and the white head with a broad dark stripe through the eye are particularly noticeable. In flight, the underwing is pale with dark marks at the bend. The wings are long and slender, and held so that they slope first up and then down to the tips – like a very flattened letter M. Ospreys mostly breed near lakes or slow-flowing rivers, and feed on fish which they catch by flying, fairly slowly, low over the water, stopping to circle and hover when prey is sighted just below the surface, and finally dropping feet first to grasp it in the talons. Because of their habitat and coloration, confusion with large gulls is possible. Summer visitors to Scotland, Norway, Sweden and eastward from northern Germany, ospreys are resident in parts of the Mediterranean area. They may occur throughout northern Europe on migration.

Golden Eagle *Aquila chrysaetos* L 75–88cm

Eagle and buzzard identification can be difficult. All have high-pitched, mewing calls and they are usually seen far off, characteristically soaring in rising air currents. To manage this efficiently, they have evolved broad wings and tails and thus look similar, although there are some differences in shape and flying style. However, where one species occurs, others are often absent. Golden eagles are massive, with exceptionally wide wings and tail – the 'flying door' description is quite appropriate. Juveniles have white patches on wings and tails, reducing as they mature, and turn into dark brown adults with golden heads. Superb aviators, they can cover distance very fast with leisurely flaps and glides, diving on prey with wings folded back. Holding vast hunting territories, golden eagles live in hill and mountain country, taking birds and medium-sized mammals, plus carrion. They are resident in northern Britain, Norway, Spain and southeast Europe, and are found as winter visitors in Sweden and Denmark.

Buzzard *Buteo buteo* L 50–55cm [middle] / **Honey Buzzard** *Pernis apivorus* L 50–58cm [bottom]

Buzzards and honey buzzards are much smaller than golden eagles, although they appear large when compared with most other species. Both buzzards and honey buzzards have very variable plumage; most are brown with paler underparts, but some are very pale and others are uniformly dark. Honey buzzards have small, almost pigeon-like heads which are often apparent in flight, when another point to notice is the tail pattern – two bars near the base and a broad bar at the tip on typical individuals. By contrast, buzzards have shorter tails with even barring. In both species there is usually a noticeable dark mark on the underside of each wing at the carpal joint, and honey buzzards sometimes have dark lines running the length of the wings. Often habitat and behaviour are better identification guides than plumage. Buzzards feed on live prey, mostly large insects and mammals up to rabbit size, and they use a wide variety of habitats. They are much commoner than golden eagles and much more widely distributed in the nesting season than honey buzzards, which breed in extensive deciduous woodland where they feed mainly on the larvae of wasps and bees, digging out the nests with their strong feet and sometimes excavating such deep holes that they disappear below ground level. Honey buzzards are only present in Europe in summer, being absent from Ireland and very rare in Britain and Norway. Buzzards, however, are resident over all western and central Europe, although absent in much of lowland England and Ireland; they also occur in Scandinavia in summer. A third species, the rough-legged buzzard *(Buteo lagopus)*, breeds in much of Scandinavia and migrates south in winter, when it may occur in Britain, the Low Countries and Germany. Always a pale bird, it has a very light underwing with dark patches at the angle, and a pale tail with a black terminal bar. It also hovers more frequently than either buzzards or honey buzzards.

Red Kite *Milvus milvus* L 61 cm

Red kites are a light rufous colour with pale heads, and in flight they reveal large pale patches on the underwings close to the black wingtips. Both buoyant flying style and silhouette are distinctive. The wings are long, slender and usually angled back at the ends. The tail is long, deeply notched and often flexed. Kites given an impression of feeling and responding to air currents much more sentitively than buzzards. Although well known for carrion feeding, red kites also take many sorts of small creatures. Their preferred breeding habitat is broad-leaved woodland in which to nest, close to open country where they can hunt. For various reasons, kites have diminished over much of their former range. In Britain the total population is under thirty pairs, all in Wales. They are resident in southern Europe and occur as summer visitors as far north as southern Sweden.

Kestrel *Falco tinnunculus* L 34 cm

Having evolved as high-speed interceptors, all falcons have long, pointed wings and long tails. Like most other birds of prey, they have large heads to contain the large eyes necessary for detecting prey, and a powerful beak. Kestrels are the commonest European falcons, and once familiar with them identification of other species is easier. The male's contrasting grey-and-brown coloration is unmistakable. Females and young have heavily barred brown plumage and may at first be confused with other birds, including cuckoos, but the hunting technique of prolonged hovering is most distinctive as the kestrel searches for voles and large insects in rough grassland and open ground. Birds are also taken, notably in towns where kestrels occasionally nest on buildings. Elsewhere they breed in trees, on crags and on cliffs. The species is resident throughout Europe except northern Scandinavia where it is a summer migrant.

Hobby *Falco subbuteo* L 30–36 cm

Adult hobbies are slate-backed with a dark crown and moustachial stripes which contrast with the white cheeks. These make good long-distance identification features. The reddish thighs and undertail show up at close range. Immatures are browner overall, without the reddish underparts. Hobbies feed on large insects, swallows, martins and even swifts caught in flight, and they can travel very fast indeed. With long, curved-back wings and a shorter tail than the kestrel, a hobby flashing across the sky often looks in silhouette remarkably like a giant swift itself. Favouring rather open country — downland, heaths and park-like landscapes, with scattered clumps of trees in which to nest, hobbies often hunt near open water, where they can find both dragonflies and hirundines (swallows and martins) catching small insects. They are summer visitors to Europe as far north as southern England and Sweden.

Peregrine Falcon *Falco peregrinus* L 38–48cm

The female peregrine falcon is substantially bigger than the male, and both sexes have proportionately broader wings and a more robust build than any smaller falcon. Both are dark grey above and finely barred below, juvenile birds being dark brown with streaked underparts. Peregrine falcons feed on birds up to the size of pigeons and grouse. Like other raptors, they will spend long periods sitting and waiting for prey to come into range, but they will also 'wait on' at high altitude and then stoop at speed with nearly closed wings at a bird below, striking it with the talons in passing and often pulling up and catching the falling victim before it hits the ground. They nest on undisturbed upland crags and sea-cliffs. Many winter on estuaries, where waders provide plentiful food. Once breeding throughout Europe, peregrine falcons are much reduced by pesticides and Britain, where recovery is occurring, is now the major stronghold.

Merlin *Falco columbarius* L 27–33cm

The male merlin is grey above with streaked, warm-brown underparts and is smaller than the hen which is brown with a heavily barred tail; juveniles resemble females. Both sexes lack the distinct moustaches of peregrine falcon, hobby and kestrel. Smallest of the European falcons, merlins are birds of open heather moorland and tundra, using rocks or posts as observation points – a common habit in birds of prey. They usually hunt at low altitude, pursuing pipits and other small birds and giving an impression of great speed and manoeuvrability. The nest may be on the ground or in a tree when, like kestrels and hobbies, they use the old nests of other birds. Resident in suitable habitats in Britain and Ireland, and summer visitors to Norway and Sweden, merlins are found elsewhere in Europe only in winter when, at least in some areas, they particularly favour coastal marshes and estuaries.

Sparrowhawk *Accipiter nisus* L 28–38cm

While falcons hunt in open country, hawks are woodland predators whose long tails and rounded wings give them the ability to dash and weave through cover. The rounded wings are not always a reliable identification guide, as all birds of prey can vary wing shape depending on the mode of flight; however, habitat is a good clue, even with a brief view. The male sparrowhawk is bluish-brown above with rufous barring below, and the appreciably larger female is brown above with brown barrings. Young birds are also brown but have speckled breasts.

Goshawks *(Accipiter gentilis)* have a similar build and markings but are much larger – they look like long-tailed, short-winged buzzards – and are generally uncommon. Sparrowhawks are widespread in woodland, scrub and hedgerow country, where females catch birds of up to thrush size, and males prey mainly on tits and finches. They are resident throughout Europe except northern Scandinavia which they visit only in summer.

Cuckoo *Cuculus canorus* L 33cm

Both adults and young cuckoos can be mistaken at first for hawks or falcons, but closer examination reveals that the beak is longer and not hooked, and the tail has a very rounded end and is white spotted. Some cuckoos are brown and not grey. Flight and behaviour are characteristic; in the air they keep their pointed wings low, weakly flapping them below the level of the body; they usually perch horizontally, unlike birds of prey which sit upright. The male's familiar 'cooc-ooo' and the noisy coughing and bubbling notes of both sexes are immediately recognizable. Cuckoos are brood parasites, the female laying single eggs in the nests of small birds such as dunnocks and meadow pipits; as soon as the young cuckoo hatches, it ejects the rightful eggs or young and is reared by its foster-parents. Cuckoos are summer visitors to all Europe, occurring in most habitats.

Nightjar *Caprimulgus europaeus* L 27cm

Largely active at dusk and after dark, nightjars are best known for their prolonged, churring song which has sudden changes in pitch, unlike the unvaried reeling of the grasshopper warbler. The flight call is a nasal 'coo-ik'. If seen, they appear as long-winged, long-tailed birds reminiscent of falcons and with an agile, floating flight. The male has two white spots on the corners of the tail and white marks on the outer wing. Nightjars rest by day, closing their eyes to mere slits. When at the nest on the ground, the camouflaged plumage blends with its background, and when perched the bird turns to squat parallel with a bough and so looks like the stump of a broken branch. Living on insects, especially moths caught in flight, nightjars are widely but patchily distributed in Europe and occur only in summer, preferring woodland clearings, heaths and open country with few trees.

Wryneck *Jynx torquilla* L 16.5cm

The wryneck is a shy species, often overlooked even where it is not uncommon, but given a reasonable view it is not easily confused with any other bird. The plumage is remarkably beautiful in elegantly subdued shades of brown and lilac-grey, darker on the upperparts and finely barred beneath. The dark stripe down the back is a noticeable feature and the bird sometimes raises its head feathers in a short crest. Ants are the wryneck's principal food and it mainly hunts them on the ground, hopping about with its barred tail raised, although it can cling to tree trunks like the related woodpeckers. It often swivels its head to odd angles; perhaps this trick is helpful in the pursuit of its small and scurrying prey. The preferred habitat is mature deciduous woodland with open glades and its summer range covers most of Europe, except northern Scandinavia. In Britain only a handful now breed.

Green Woodpecker *Picus viridis* L 32cm

All woodpeckers are shy birds, and the green woodpecker will quietly fly off at the approach of a human, or slip discreetly round the other side of the branch. Often the loud and ringing laugh is a first clue to its presence, or you may have a glimpse of the bird's green wings and bright yellow rump as it flies off. Like other woodpeckers, it has a very bounding flight. Green woodpeckers often feed on the ground, particularly excavating ants' nests. They occur in all sorts of well-wooded areas, but not in exclusively coniferous woodlands. They are residents throughout Europe, excluding Ireland, north Britain and northern Scandinavia. The closely related grey-headed woodpecker *(Picus canus)* occurs in a broad belt stretching east from western France and into part of Norway and Sweden. Both sexes have grey heads, the males with a small red patch on the forehead.

Great Spotted Woodpecker *Dendrocopos major* L 23cm

The great spotted woodpecker is a black-and-white bird with a red patch under the tail: males also have a small red bar across the back of the head and young birds have wholly red crowns. There is a large white patch where each wing joins the body. Hidden in the treetops, a feeding great spotted wood-pecker often first reveals itself by its tapping on a branch   pine cone, or by the call — a sharp 'tchick'. In spring, the song is made by drumming loudly and rapidly for about a second at a time on a resonating bough. Great spotted woodpeckers are resident over all of Europe, excluding Ireland and the more northern parts of Norway. They occur in fairly mature deciduous and coniferous woodland, feeding on insects that live on and beneath bark, as well as on tree seeds. The central European middle spotted woodpecker *(Dendrocopos medius)* is more compact with an all-red crown.

Lesser Spotted Woodpecker *Dendrocopos minor* L 14.5cm

No larger than sparrows, and feeding among the upper branches of trees, lesser spotted woodpeckers are easily missed. In spring, they drum less loudly than great spotted woodpeckers, but in more prolonged bursts of ten to twenty blows, lasting for about two seconds. The male has a red cap but the female is entirely black and white. The back and wings are barred with white, and lesser spotted woodpeckers lack the large white shoulder patches of great spotted woodpeckers. Absent from Ireland and northern Britain, but otherwise wide-spread residents in Europe, they are associated with deciduous woodland and often found where the trees are old and widely spaced, such as in orchards and riverside alders. The nest-hole is usually excavated in a branch rather than on the trunk as with other woodpeckers. Frequently found alongside great spotted woodpeckers, they feed in different parts of the trees and thus do not compete.

Golden Oriole *Oriolus oriolus* L 24cm

The male golden oriole is an unmistakable bird, with its golden-yellow body contrasting with black wings and upper tail. Some females are also yellow but most, like the juveniles, have a greenish head, back and tail, speckled under-parts and greyish wings: thus there is some possibility of confusion with green woodpeckers, the more so as both species have undulating flights. Despite the male's bright colours, it is often as hard to see in the treetops as the more evidently camouflaged female, and both sexes are rather secretive, eyeing you cautiously through a screen of leaves. Often it is the male's fluting 'or-ee-ole' song or a cat-like squalling note that reveals its presence. Orioles breed in broadleaved wood and parkland, feeding on large insects plus some fruit, and rarely descending out of the trees. They are summer visitors to Europe, occurring only rarely in the British Isles and Scandinavia.

Hoopoe *Upupa epops* L 28cm

The hoopoe has a pinkish-brown head and underparts, contrasting with the pied back and tail. The crest is often folded down. In its somewhat butterfly-like flight, the predominant impression is of a bird with black wings and tail, both strongly barred with white. Despite their distinctive appearance, hoopoes are sometimes confused with jays, which share a slightly similar pink-and-pied appearance; however, jays have far less white on their wings, which are not nearly so broad and rounded. The call is a low but carrying 'poo-poo-poo'. Hoopoes feed mainly on insects and invertebrates living in the soil, which they probe with their long beaks. They favour warm, dry regions and are found on farmland, in gardens and in open woodland. Nesting in holes, they occur in Europe as summer visitors, most commonly in the south, and are only rarely seen in the British Isles and Scandinavia.

Jay *Garrulus glandarius* L 34cm

Jays are difficult to see well because they live mainly in woodland, and are very wary birds indeed. They have a scolding alarm screech which sounds like violently tearing linen. The usual view of a jay is as it slips away through the trees, giving the impression of a medium-sized pinkish bird with dark wings and tail and a conspicuous white rump. Occasionally jays will be seen flying between woodlands, and they always look as if they find it hard work, flapping weakly and erratically. The blue feathers on the wings are most noticeable when the bird is at rest. Jays take insects, seeds, eggs and young birds. They bury acorns in autumn and not all of these are subsequently found and eaten, so that jays play an important role in the regeneration of oakwoods. They are resident throughout Europe excluding parts of Ireland, Scotland and northern Scandinavia.

Raven *Corvus corax* L 64cm

Identifying the large, black members of the crow family is often not easy and care must be taken to distinguish ravens from carrion crows. Although they are very large birds – as big as buzzards – this is not always obvious at long range, and points to look for are the massive beak and large head, extending well forward in flight, and the long, wedge-ended tail. The wings are long and relatively slender, so that the birds often appear cross-shaped in the air. Ravens perform superb aerobatics, somersaulting and diving, often apparently for the sheer fun of it. Their usual call is a deep croaking 'pro-ak'. Taking a very wide range of food, they can live in almost all habitats but, due to human persecution, have a discontinuous distribution. They are largely absent from France, Germany, Belgium and Holland and from lowland Britain and Ireland, but occur as residents throughout the rest of Europe.

Carrion Crow [illustrated]/**Hooded Crow** *Corvus corone* L 47cm

Carrion crows are smaller and less powerfully beaked than ravens, and they lack the white face-patch and shaggy 'trousers' of adult rooks. They are also much less sociable birds than rooks and are most likely to be seen singly, in pairs or at the end of the breeding season in family parties, but flocks are rare except at communal winter roosts. The distribution covers almost all sorts of habitats throughout western Europe, except Ireland, north Scotland, Scandinavia and Italy. In these areas they are replaced by a closely related bird, the hooded crow, which has a brownish-grey body with black head, wings and tail. The hooded crow's habits and behaviour are the same as the carrion crow's and, where the ranges of the two birds meet, they interbreed so that hybrid forms occur. Some hooded crows winter over much of the range of the carrion crow.

Rook *Corvus frugilegus* L 46cm

Usually rooks are seen in parties, as they nest and feed communally. The same size as carrion crows, they are distinguished by the white face-patch of the adults and by the heavily feathered upper legs. As well as their familiar cawing, they have some rather high-pitched and gull-like calls. Breeding colonies are established for preference in the tops of mature trees, and the birds return to the same site for many years unless seriously persecuted. In winter, rooks and jackdaws flock together and great numbers may gather in secure roosts. Because they feed mainly on worms, insects and other soil invertebrates, as well as plant matter, rooks are much more associated with farmland or other areas of soft ground than are crows. They are resident throughout the British Isles and across northern Europe, excluding most of Norway and Sweden, but birds from areas where soils are frozen in winter migrate south.

Jackdaw *Corvus monedula* L 33cm

As well as being substantially smaller than crows and rooks, the jackdaw has a grey nape, usually easily seen. In flight the wing-beats are faster than those of the larger members of the family. Their calls are higher pitched and shorter than rook or crows — variations on 'chak' and 'kow'. Jackdaws are hole-nesting birds, using cavities in old trees or rocks, in buildings or ruins and chimney pots. They usually breed in colonies and, like rooks, will feed and flock to winter roosts in large parties. Taking a wide range of food, they occur in fairly open country particularly farmland with livestock, where large soil inverte-brates and insects are more numerous than in arable land (this also applies to rooks). They are widely distributed and resident over all of Europe, but on the northern edge of their range in southern Sweden and Norway, jackdaws are migratory.

Magpie *Pica pica* L 46cm

Their strongly pied appearance and very long tails make magpies easy to recognize. At close range you can see that the apparently black plumage is in fact a mixture of metallic blues and greens. Despite their striking looks, magpies can be surprisingly hard to see, as they are wary birds and in some localities will discreetly vanish into cover when a human approaches. Because of this, they manage to survive well in most areas, even though intensely disliked by game-rearing interests due to their skill in finding nests and taking the eggs and young of other birds. Like most other members of the family, magpies will eat a wide variety of food. Their usual call is a hard, rapid rattling 'sha-sha-sha-shak'. The nest is a large domed structure of thorny twigs, usually placed in a low tree or bush. Magpies are resident over all of Europe, except northern Scotland.

Swift *Apus apus* L 16.5cm

Swifts live an almost entirely aerial existence, alighting only to nest, lay eggs and rear their young. Apparently they usually sleep on the wing, rising to high altitude at dusk, and they are adapted for sustained high-speed flight with narrow swept-back wings and streamlined bodies. The plumage is almost black, with a barely visible whitish throat-patch. Swallows and martins are somewhat similarly shaped, but all have pale underparts, shorter wings and less rapid flight. Swifts cannot perch, but have hooked toes with which they can cling to walls and so crawl into the sheltered cavities, such as gaps in church towers or the eaves of old houses, where they nest. They are particularly associated with towns, where groups of them may be seen whirling and screaming noisily around the buildings. Feeding on insects, swifts are summer visitors to all but the northernmost parts of Europe.

Swallow *Hirundo rustica* L 19cm

Living on insects caught in flight, swallows and martins are rapid flyers. They have longish, swept-back wings and have a superficial resemblance to swifts, but are much less completely adapted to an aerial existence. They will perch regularly, most noticeably on telegraph wires where they may gather in excited, twittering parties prior to migration. Swallows have uniformly dark blue backs and brick-red faces, the underparts are largely pale and the very long tail-streamers are quite distinctive. Young birds, however, have shorter, notched tails and could be confused with martins. The cup-shaped nest is built of mud pellets collected from wet ground and placed on a ledge, always in a situation where it is under cover and almost invariably in a building such as an outhouse or stable. Mostly seen flying low over open country, swallows are summer visitors to all of Europe except the extreme north.

House Martin *Delichon urbica* L 12.5cm

Smaller than swallows, house martins have shorter wings, rather plump cylindrical bodies and short, notched tails without long tail-streamers. They are a dark metallic blue above, with a conspicuous white rump and underparts. The nest is built of mud pellets and completely enclosed except for a small entrance-hole at the top. Their natural nest sites, where some may still be found, were on the walls of cliffs and open caves, but nowadays most birds attach their nests in the angle under the eaves of houses or on other buildings, including bridges. The adoption of this habit, like the swallow's use of barns and outbuildings, must have enabled both species to greatly increase in numbers as far more artificial sites exist than were ever available naturally. Unlike swallows, martins normally nest colonially and often build side by side. They occur as summer migrants to the whole of Europe.

Sand Martin *Riparia riparia* L 12cm

Sand martins are uniformly brown above with a broad brown chest band across the white underparts. Their tails are short and only slightly notched and they appear much shorter-winged and less streamlined than swallows. Occurring as summer visitors throughout Europe, sand martins breed colonially, nesting in closely spaced burrows which they excavate in the vertical banks of rivers and sand or gravel pits. The modern demand for these minerals has greatly increased the available habitat and although sites are often destroyed, the birds readily move to new locations. As the nesting colonies are usually sited close to water, sand martins tend to feed over it even more than swallows and house martins, but in autumn all three species often occur in large numbers at ponds and lakes. Where there are reed beds, they may use these as communal roosting places until they depart for the winter.

Great Grey Shrike *Lanius excubitor* L 24cm [illustrated]/**Lesser Grey Shrike** *Lanius minor* L 20cm

These species are only likely to be confused with each other, and then only in southern Europe in summer, when the two overlap. Both are grey-bodied birds with black-and-white wings and tail. The great grey shrike has black eye-patches running back from the beak, and in the lesser grey shrike they meet in a broad band across the forehead. In flight, great grey shrikes appear to have shorter, broader and more rounded wings and longer tails. Young birds of both species are brownish. They live in open woodland or among scattered trees, eating large insects, small mammals and occasionally small birds. Great grey shrikes are present all year in most of Europe including southern Norway, but in northern Scandinavia they occur only in summer, and in southern Sweden and Britain only in winter. They are absent from Ireland. Lesser grey shrikes are summer visitors to the southern half of Europe, excluding Spain.

Red-backed Shrike *Lanius collurio* L 17cm

The male red-backed shrike is instantly recognizable; a rather brightly coloured bird with blue-grey head and rump, heavy black eyestripe, chestnut back and wings, pinkish underparts and black tail. The female is much duller — uniform brown above with a faint eyestripe, and pale below with fine barring. Juveniles are like her, but have more mottled backs and may be confused with young woodchat shrikes. However, there is no problem in separating shrikes from all similar birds as they have characteristic, powerful beaks. Red-backed shrikes are often common breeding birds in open scrub country and along hedgerows. Like other shrikes, they tend to perch on the tops or outsides of bushes or trees to watch out for the large insects and lizards on which they mainly feed. Their summer range extends from northern Spain throughout Europe into the south of Sweden and southern England, where they are now very rare.

Woodchat Shrike *Lanius senator* L 17cm

Adult woodchat shrikes are superficially similar to pied flycatchers, sharing with them a habit of perching in exposed positions, but note that they have chestnut caps and pale rumps as well as the heavy, hooked shrike's beak. In flight the upper wings are black with white flashes near the tips, and white stripes like braces run down over the shoulders and back, to join the white rump, which itself continues as a white border round the black tail. Juveniles are brown, but faintly show the same basic distribution of light and dark patterning as in the adults. Woodchats inhabit open woodland, scrub and roadsides where there are trees or wires from which to watch for prey — all sorts of small animals, taken mainly on the ground. They are summer migrants to southern and western Europe, north nearly to the Channel coast and into northern Germany.

Kingfisher *Alcedo atthis* L 16.5cm

Kingfishers are very brilliantly coloured, the iridescent blue upperparts contrasting with the bright chestnut plumage below. Despite this, they are easily overlooked as they sit still or fly rapidly, direct and low over the water. Fortunately they call fairly often, and the shrill, piping 'chee' is a forewarning of the fleeting blue flash of a passing bird. The nest is made at the end of a tunnel excavated by both adults in a soil bank, but not always by the water. Kingfishers are resident throughout Europe except Norway, most of Sweden and north Britain. Feeding on fish caught by diving, usually from a perch but sometimes after hovering, kingfishers are found in many freshwater habitats and, during the winter months, may also be seen on the coast and in estuaries. They are very vulnerable to freezing conditions which prevent their feeding, so that large numbers die in prolonged icy weather.

Dipper *Cinclus cinclus* L 18cm

A plump and short-tailed brown bird with a white breast, the dipper presents no identification problem. The young birds are grey above and pale below with dark, scaly markings, but their build, habitat and behaviour will always identify them. Dippers have evolved to exploit a habitat which no other bird uses – the beds of fast-flowing, clear streams. They can swim and dive well, walking along the bottom and probing around and under stones to seek all sorts of small creatures, mostly insect larvae but also water snails, tadpoles and fish fry. They fly low and fast, usually following the course of the stream, and are most likely to be seen perched on a projecting rock, when their plumage is quite good camouflage among the brown boulders and white water. They are resident over most of western Europe but rarely occur in the lowlands, where little suitable habitat exists.

Waxwing *Bombycilla garrulus* L 18cm

Waxwings are beautiful birds, unmistakable except in flight when they look rather like starlings. Young birds are much browner, without the bright spots of colour and with streaky underparts, but have the same distinctive shape as adults. Waxwings breed in northern forests of birch and conifer, occurring all year round in the far north of Scandinavia. A proportion of the population moves south each winter, some reaching western Europe, including the British Isles, France and Germany. Periodically this species 'erupts' from its breeding areas in great numbers, and may be locally numerous in places where it has not been seen for years. In their wintering areas, waxwings feed exclusively on berries and fruit, and may be found on hawthorn bushes and ornamental shrubs, or in orchards where apples remain on the trees. They exhibit surprising agility for such stocky birds, happily hanging head down to peck at the fruit, and are very confiding.

Mistle Thrush   *Turdus viscivorus*   L 27cm

Mistle thrushes are large, boldly marked birds. Bigger than song thrushes, they have more heavily spotted underparts and a generally paler, grey cast to the plumage. In flight they alternately flap and glide like fieldfares, although with a more undulating result, and they have a similarly pale underwing, but the flight and alarm call is a quite distinctive churring or rattling. The song is usually delivered from a tree top and is loud and ringing, less mellow than a blackbird's and less repetitive than a song thrush's; mistle thrushes start to sing earlier in the year than most other species. They live in broadleaved woodland, as well as farmland and other areas with trees. Family parties will be seen in late summer but mistle thrushes rarely flock in winter. They are resident throughout Europe and into southern Sweden, but further north occur only in summer and are largely absent from Norway.

Song Thrush   *Turdus philomelos*   L 23cm

As with the other thrush species described here, male and female song thrushes are identical. They are smaller than mistle thrushes, with a warmer brown colouring and less heavy spotting on the breast. The underwing is buffish orange and can look quite bright, but is not nearly so strongly russet as in the redwing. The flight is direct with continuous flapping – like redwing, but unlike mistle thrush and fieldfare. Song thrushes have pleasant but repetitive songs, often whistling the same few notes twice in succession; a common phrase may be rendered as 'pretty joey, pretty joey. . . .'. The alarm note is a run-together clucking shriek, rather like the blackbird's. Basically birds of woodland, they also occur on farmland with hedges and in suburban situations in much of Europe. Song thrushes are present all year in Europe east to Germany, where they occur only as summer visitors, most birds also leaving Scandinavia in the winter.

Redwing   *Turdus iliacus*   L 21cm

Redwings are usually easily identified. The facial stripes stand out against the dark brown head, and the flanks and underwing are strongly marked with russet-red, visible both when the birds are perched and in flight. The song is briefer and simpler than the song thrush's. The usual flight note is a rather faint, lisping 'seeh'; often when redwing are migrating at night you may hear this call as the invisible flock passes overhead. They are a northerly breeding species, occurring in Norway, Sweden and, as recent colonists, in Scotland. They generally live in more open woodland than song thrushes. Interestingly, although song thrushes are garden birds elsewhere in Europe, redwings replace them in town gardens in Scandinavia. The winter range extends from southern Norway and the British Isles southward to the Mediterranean; redwings live at this season mainly on farmland and feed especially on hedgerow berries.

Fieldfare *Turdus pilaris* L 25.5cm

A large thrush, the fieldfare has a distinctive grey head and rump, a dark tail and a warm-brown back. Like the mistle thrush, it has a characteristic flight, flapping several times and then briefly closing its wings and shooting forward before flapping again: despite this, the flight is not noticeably undulating but strong and direct. The two species have different calls, the fieldfare's being a loud, repeated 'tchak, tchak'. Fieldfares breed in light woodland, especially with birch and pine, being found year-round from eastern France through Germany, as well as in all but central Norway and Sweden which they visit only during the breeding season. Small numbers have recently colonized Belgium, Holland, Denmark and Britain. In winter they occur throughout almost all of Europe, often in large flocks together with redwings, and feed on mainly open farmland.

Blackbird *Turdus merula* L 25cm

A sleek black bird with orange beak and eye ring, in most situations a male blackbird cannot be confused with any other species. Females and young are brown, darker on the back and indistinctly streaked beneath — much more brown overall than any thrush. In flight, blackbirds have much longer tails than starlings, for which they might otherwise be mistaken. The song is unusually mellow and flowing, without the repeated phrases which are a feature of the song thrush's performance. When flushed, blackbirds fly off with a hysterical, chattering screech and when mobbing a predator or settling to roost for the night, they make a repeated metallic 'chink, chink'. Found in a wide variety of habitats including woods, farms, gardens and towns, blackbirds feed on many sorts of fruits and invertebrates. They are resident over all Europe north as far as southern Scandinavia, occurring as summer migrants in central Norway and Sweden.

Ring Ouzel *Turdus torquatus* L 24cm

The male ring ouzel looks rather like a male blackbird with a broad white throat-patch and pale wing-patches, and the hen resembles a female blackbird, being brown with the same white markings as her mate, although these are less well defined. The song is very simple, a slow repetition of two or three beautifully fluty notes which carry a surprisingly long way. Ring ouzels are upland birds, associated with lightly wooded or open country such as moor, heath or mountain provided there is some cover; often they will be found where there are crags or rocky outcrops and some stunted trees or bushes. They breed in the Pyrenees and Alps, in the upland parts of the British Isles and in Sweden and Norway, (progressively occurring at lower altitudes the further north they nest). They may be seen on migration throughout central Europe, and some birds winter in southern France and Spain.

Starling *Sturnus vulgaris* L 21.5cm

Starlings have low crowns, stout bodies and short tails. In summer, the plumage has an iridescent, purple-green sheen and the beak is yellow. In winter it is browner, with copious white spots. Young birds are very brown and unspotted, but have the same shape and bustling, 'hands-in-pockets' gait as adults. Starlings have a characteristic, rather triangular shape in flight. The cheerful song often contains many phrases mimicked from other birds such as song thrushes and lapwings; sometimes, you can guess the starling's winter habitat by the calls it uses in spring. Hole nesters, starlings breed in woodland, cliffs and around buildings. They feed on open ground, often flocking on farm and moor, and occurring in vast winter roosts in city centres and in woods. They are present all year in western Europe, but visit northern Scandinavia only in summer. Some winter in Spain, where the aptly named spotless starling *(Sturnus unicolor)* breeds.

Bluethroat *Luscinia svecica* L 14cm

Two forms of bluethroat breed in Europe. In Scandinavia, the male has a red spot in the centre of his blue throat-patch, but in central Europe the spot is white. Females usually have white throats but with a dark band across the upper chest as in males. Both sexes have a conspicuous pale eyestripe and orange patches on the base of the dark tail, best seen when the bird is in flight; the speckled juvenile shares this feature. Robin-like in shape and posture, bluethroats are secretive birds feeding close to the ground in cover, where they are often difficult to see. They prefer swampy woodland and have a patchy breeding distribution, occurring in central Spain, western France and from eastern France through Germany into eastern Europe, as well as in Norway and part of Sweden. Birds occur on passage over a wide area including eastern Britain, and some winter in Spain.

Robin *Erithacus rubecula* L 14cm

Robins are very well known and need little description, but it is worth noting that the red coloration extends up on to the face, as this is not the case in any other red-chested European bird. Juvenile robins have mottled backs and rather scaly looking brown underparts, but they have the characteristic rather plump and round-headed robin shape, the same upright stance, often with slightly drooped wings, and the same enquiring tilt of the head as they scan the ground for food. The song is a pleasant warbling with a very distinctive tone, and robins also have an easily identified ticking call. Essentially woodland birds, where they have learnt to pick up insects and other invertebrates from ground disturbed by large mammals, in some countries robins are also widespread in gardens and parks. They are resident throughout Europe except Norway and Sweden where they occur as summer visitors.

Redstart *Phoenicurus phoenicurus* L 14cm

A male redstart in breeding plumage is a very striking bird with a red breast, black face, white forehead and grey back. The most important identification point for all redstarts is the red tail, which is constantly flicked up and down. Young and winter males are duller versions of the adult male in summer plumage, while female and juvenile birds are rather nondescript, being brownish above and fawn below; somewhat like nightingales but with much redder tails. Redstarts are mainly birds of mature broadleaved woodland, but sometimes occur in pines or where there are scattered trees, the important requirement being old timber with holes in which to nest. Their most usual call is easily recognized as it consists of a squeaky whistle and two ticks, 'whee, tic-tic'. They are summer visitors to all Europe including the extreme north, but are extremely rare in Ireland and have a very patchy distribution in Britain.

Black Redstart *Phoenicurus ochruros* L 14cm

Black redstarts share the red tail of the common redstart but are much darker coloured. The male is a sooty black, usually with a whitish patch on the wings, but this is often obscure. Female and young are rather uniformly dark brown above and below, unlike the paler common redstarts. On migration both species may occur together, but their breeding habitats are quite different. Black redstarts prefer rocky situations and are also associated with houses or other buildings. They have extended their European range this century, in some areas almost entirely by living around industrial complexes such as warehouses and power stations. Resident in parts of southern Europe and also in western France, they are summer visitors to the rest of Europe north to Denmark, and occur as a rare breeding species in Sweden as well as in the south of England where some birds also overwinter.

Nightingale *Luscinia megarhynchos* L 16.5cm

The nightingale is a rather uniformly brown bird with pale underparts and a rufous tail which may cause it to be confused with young redstarts. However, redstarts' tails are much brighter red, and they are somewhat smaller birds. Generally, nightingales are not readily seen, as they are a skulking species, feeding and singing in cover. The song is a remarkably rich and varied fluting. It includes a number of easily recognized phrases, including a bubbling 'chook-chook-chook' and a drawn-out repeated 'pioo', rising in crescendo to a high-pitched trill. It may be heard throughout the day as well as at night. Nightingales live in thickets of bush or scrub and in broadleaved woodland, provided there is plenty of low cover beneath which they feed on insects, other invertebrates and berries. They are summer migrants breeding through-out Europe north as far as southern Britain and Denmark.

Stonechat *Saxicola torquata* L 12.5cm

The black or dark brown head and face, together with the rufous chest, separate the male stonechat from any other species. Female and young are a much paler mottled brown on the head, chin and back, but lack the white eyestripe and orange-buff chin, the pale underparts and white tail-patches of the whinchat. Stonechats are very short-tailed birds, with particularly round heads, and they habitually perch on the tops of bushes and fences. The usual call is a repeated chacking note, rather like that of other chats and wheatears. Stonechats are primarily birds of gorse heath and moorland with scattered bushes or trees, and they are often commonest in mild coastal situations. They are resident over much of the extreme west and south of Europe but from central France eastward occur only as summer visitors; they are absent from Norway and Sweden.

Whinchat *Saxicola rubetra* L 12.5cm

The male whinchat is mottled brown above with dull orange underparts. The white stripes over the eye and across the wing are conspicuous identification features. Female and young are paler versions of the male with fainter (although still evident) eyestripes, and all whinchats have white patches on each side of the tail which are especially conspicuous when landing. Confusion of whinchats with hen stonechats is possible, but stonechats lack eystripes, are duller with reddish brown underparts and have a distinctively round-headed appearance. Whinchats prefer rough grassland, ideally with low bushes to provide songposts, although failing them, tall weeds or fences will serve. They are restless little birds and their ticking call and use of conspicuous perches make them fairly easy to spot wherever they occur. Feeding on insects, they are summer visitors to all Europe except the extreme north and most of Ireland, wintering in Africa.

Wheatear *Oenanthe oenanthe* L 14.5cm

Often, the first sight of a wheatear is when the white patch on the rump catches your eye as the bird bobs ahead low over the ground, to settle with an upright stance on a rock or mound. The male bird is grey-backed with a conspicuous white rump, black cheek stripe, wings and tail-tip, and orange-brown chest. Females and young are much browner birds overall but they share the distinctive white rump and black-tipped tail. There are no other similar species seen often in northern Europe. Wheatears are birds of open country, such as grassland, heath, moor and tundra. They rarely perch off the ground and they nest in rock cavities, holes in dry walls and, quite often, rabbit burrows. Their calls are a grating 'chak, chak', sometimes preceded by a squeaky, whistled note — 'wheet, chak-chak'. They occur in suitable habitats throughout Europe as summer visitors.

Spotted Flycatcher *Muscicapa striata* L 14cm

Male and female spotted flycatchers are identical. They are small, grey-brown birds with darker streaks on the crown and breast, although these are not always very obvious as the underparts can be rather grey. They are instantly identifiable by their very upright way of perching and by their mode of feeding. They use a perch in an exposed position giving a good all-round view, rather than inside a bush or tree as most birds do, and from this point they fly swiftly out to capture passing insects, usually returning at once to their starting point. Other birds also 'flycatch', including warblers and sparrows, but none do so habitually and they rarely use a fixed hunting perch. Spotted flycatchers are found in all sorts of wooded and semi-wooded situations, provided there are open clearings, including hedges with trees and large gardens. They are summer visitors to all of Europe.

Pied Flycatcher *Ficedula hypoleuca* L 13cm

In summer plumage, a male pied flycatcher is white below and black above with large white patches on the wings and tail, and a small white mark on the forehead. Females, young birds and males in winter are much duller – grey-brown above and pale-fawn below – but all have some white marking on the wings and tail. Usually their behaviour readily identifies them. Like other flycatchers they have a rather upright stance and habitually perch on vantage points, from which they can catch small insects on the wing. Pied flycatchers also pick food from the ground and from leaves. They are summer visitors to areas with open woodland or clumps of trees throughout Europe, but are absent from Ireland, much of lowland Britain and most of France. In parts of central and southern Europe the collared flycatcher *(Ficedula albicollis)* occurs and is distinguished mainly by the white band round the back of the male's neck.

Dunnock *Prunella modularis* L 14.5cm

Usually a very inconspicuous bird, the dunnock spends much time on the ground, creeping about and picking up tiny creatures and seeds. This behaviour will distinguish it from any other bird, particularly hen house sparrows and young robins, both of which, in their different ways, have a much more bouncy appearance. Although not brightly coloured, the plumage is attractive with a grey head and chest, warm brown back and brown streaked flanks. The usual call is a quite loud and high-pitched 'tseep', sometimes persistently repeated. Juveniles lack the grey colouring and are much more uniformly streaked but have the same habits as adults. Dunnocks are birds of woodland with low vegetation, hedgerows, gardens and mountain sides. They are resident over most of western and central Europe, including the extreme south of Norway and Sweden, occurring elsewhere in both countries as summer visitors only.

Wren *Troglodytes troglodytes* L 9.5cm

Wrens are almost spherical little brown birds, with tails habitually held cocked, and long, thin beaks. Their flight is whirring, usually low, from one patch of cover to another. The song is remarkably loud, prolonged and rapid, often ending in a trill, and wrens also have a vigorous churring alarm. They are much more often heard than seen, as they inhabit low vegetation and dense cover, where they feed on a wide variety of small creatures, mostly insects. Wrens are very widespread and common throughout woodland, hedges, heath and moor to coastal and suburban situations. They build covered nests made largely of moss and fitted into a cavity. During the winter, nests are used for roosting and several wrens may be found sharing the same one to reduce heat loss. They are resident over all of Europe, except northern Scandinavia, where there is some summer migration.

Nuthatch *Sitta europaea* L 14cm

Nuthatches have the unique ability to walk not only up the trunks and branches of trees, but also headfirst down them. They are plump-bodied and thick-necked, and their heads taper to long, stout and pointed beaks. Their tails are very short. The back is grey and there is a strong black line through each eye. The underparts vary from white, in the north of their range, to a rich orange-brown in the west and south. Their song is a piping, rapidly repeated 'pee, pee, pee'. Nuthatches live in woodlands, especially those with large, broad-leaved trees, where they mainly eat insects, spiders and other small creatures, picked from their hiding places in the bark. They also feed on tree fruits and nuts, which they wedge in crevices and then hammer open; occasionally they will forage on the ground. They are resident throughout Europe except Ireland, northern Britain and northern Scandinavia.

Treecreeper *Certhia familiaris* [illustrated]/**Short-toed Treecreeper** *Certhia brachydactyla* L 12.5cm

Small, mouse-like birds, treecreepers are seen hopping vertically up the trunk of a tree or along one of the main boughs and then flying down to the bottom of another and starting again. The back and tail are brown and the underparts whitish. The thin, down-curved beak is used for probing in bark crevices for tiny insects, and the tail is stiffened by strong quills so that it acts as a support for the bird as it hangs by its toes. The two species are very alike and, where their ranges overlap, they are best distinguished by habitat preference. Short-toed treecreepers are widely distributed over Europe excluding the British Isles and Scandinavia, living in broadleaved woodlands. Treecreepers occur in conifer and mixed woods over much of central and northern Europe, including Scandinavia and the British Isles; where the short-toed treecreeper is absent, they are also found in broadleaved woodlands.

Great Tit *Parus major* L 14cm

The blue-black head with conspicuous white cheeks and the yellow under-parts divided by a broad blue-black central stripe running from chin to tail, make the great tit easily recognizable even when in flight. Juvenile birds are rather brown and yellow, but their basic pattern is the same as an adult's. Great tits have a wide variety of calls, the most readily recognizable being a ringing 'see-saw, see-saw': they also make a chaffinch-like 'pink'. Living in mixed woodland, but rarely in pure conifer woods, great tits also occur on farmland where there is ample hedgerow timber, and in gardens. Like other tits they take large quantities of insects, mostly sought in trees, but they also feed extensively on the ground particularly eating seeds such as beech mast. Nesting in holes, great tits are present year round throughout all of Europe except northern Sweden and Norway where they are summer visitors.

Blue Tit *Parus caeruleus* L 11.5cm

In spring, blue tits give a general impression of being bright blue-and-yellow birds, quite unlike any other small European species, but by the end of the breeding season they may have a rather scruffy, washed-out appearance. The young birds are paler, green-yellow versions of the adults. Their song is a slightly squeaky 'tsee, tsee, tsee, tsi-si-si-si' and they have a scolding alarm. Very agile, as all tits are, they can hang upside down without difficulty, searching the boughs and foliage for insects, spiders, buds and seeds, and rarely descending to the ground. During the winter they may be found in mixed flocks with other tits, all busily moving through the largely deserted woods, their combined forces giving extra vigilance against predators such as sparrow-hawks. Blue tits are resident in mixed woodland, hedgerows and gardens throughout Europe, as far north as southern Norway and Sweden.

Long-tailed Tit *Aegithalos caudatus* L 14cm

With tails longer than their bodies, these little, fluffy pink and black birds are easily recognized. Birds in the west of Europe have black eyestripes, but those from the north and east have pure white heads. Outside the nesting season, long-tailed tits are usually seen in family parties or flocks; the usual call, heralding their approach, is a soft, puttering 'tupp', repeated every few seconds, and helping to keep all the members of the group together. Long-tailed tits breed early in the year, building domed nests often low down in bushes or brambles in the dense woodland and scrub or overgrown hedgerows which they favour. Up to twelve young may be produced, but many clutches are lost to predators and there is high mortality among all young birds before reaching maturity. Long-tailed tits are resident over much the same range as great tits and blue tits.

Coal Tit *Parus ater* L 11.5cm

The coal tit's most obvious identification feature is the white patch extending up the back of the head; in addition, it has a greyer back than the very brown marsh tits and willow tits, and two obvious wing bars. The black crown also extends down the face, often surrounding the cheek, so that from some angles they look like small, dull great tits. Their calls are varied, often thin and squeaky like those of goldcrest, and the song is a repeated 'see-too' rather like a high-pitched great tit's call. Coal tits live mainly in coniferous forests, although in the British Isles and some other areas they may also frequent mixed woodland and large gardens with ornamental firs. They feed on small insects among the pine needles and, having longer and slimmer beaks than most other tits, they can also extract the seeds from ripe cones. They are resident throughout Europe north to central Scandinavia.

Crested Tit *Parus cristatus* L 11.5cm

The small black-and-white crest is an obvious feature and, if it cannot be easily seen when the bird is in the treetops, the combination of brown coloration and white cheek with a black V-shaped mark on it will also identify a crested tit. Their most easily identifiable call is a purring trill. Crested tits are largely confined to mature conifer woodland where they feed, like coal tits, on insects and on the seeds of ripe cones. Most pairs breed in holes excavated by the female in rotting timber, as do willow tits, but natural cavities are sometimes used. Young plantations are therefore unlikely to provide sites for nesting, although the birds may feed in them. They are largely sedentary, their range extending over most of Europe except Italy, northern Scandinavia, Ireland and southern Britain; a population exists in Scotland in the Spey valley and some adjoining areas.

Marsh Tit *Parus palustris* [illustrated]/**Willow Tit** *Parus montanus* L 11.5cm

These two species are hard to separate. Each has a black cap and a small black bib under the beak, the lower half of the face and underparts are off-white and the back and tail are light brown. Most birdwatchers rely on voice to distinguish them. The marsh tit has a diagnostic 'pitch-oo' call and also a 'chicka-dee-dee-dee'. The willow tit's usual call is a very nasal buzzing 'tchair'. The two species were not separated until this century and it is doubtful if their respective ranges are yet properly known. Marsh tits are found in broadleaved woodland, while willow tits live in both conifer woods and in broadleaved woods, especially near water; however, there is considerable overlap, especially in Britain. Both species apparently occur over most of Europe except Spain, Ireland and north Britain, but marsh tits do not reach as far north in Scandinavia as willow tits.

Blackcap *Sylvia atricapilla.* L 14cm

Both male and female blackcaps have grey-brown backs and paler underparts and are identified by their distinctive caps — black in the male bird and brown in the female. The male is superficially like a marsh tit or willow tit, but lacks the white cheek and black bib and looks longer and more slender. The attractive song resembles that of the garden warbler, but may be louder and delivered in briefer snatches; distinguishing the blackcap and garden warbler by song alone is not at all easy. Blackcaps and garden warblers often occur together in woodland, although blackcaps generally inhabit more open situations, with taller trees and less dense cover, and feed higher in the canopy. They take many berries and fruit, particularly in late summer. Resident in southern and south-western countries, blackcaps are summer migrants elsewhere throughout Europe as far north as central Norway and Sweden. A few overwinter as far north as southern England.

Garden Warbler *Sylvia borin* L 14cm

With a brownish-olive back and crown, grading evenly to a paler chin and underparts, the garden warbler lacks any obvious distinguishing feature, and this fact itself is often a good indication of the bird's identity. The head is rounded and the dark eye can look quite prominent; to compensate for lack of plumage character, the song is a pleasing musical warble, very like that of the blackcap, but usually more sustained. Garden warblers live in broadleaved and coniferous woodlands, provided there is a good cover of bushes. Young conifer plantations are also suitable. The birds feed on insects picked from the leaves, and also take berries, moving unobtrusively through the cover. Summer visitors to Europe, they are rare in Ireland and northern Scotland as well as in southern Spain and Italy.

Whitethroat *Sylvia communis* L 14cm [illustrated]/**Lesser Whitethroat** *Sylvia curruca* L 13.5cm

The male whitethroat has a grey, rather pointed crown and grey cheeks contrasting distinctly with the white throat. The back is brown and the underparts are pale. Females have browner heads and cheeks, showing the same contrast with the throat patch. Confusion may arise with the lesser whitethroat which is a generally greyer bird overall, having a particularly dark cheek and lacking the whitethroat's rufous wing-patch. The whitethroat's song is a brief jangling, often uttered during a display flight between the tops of two hedgerow bushes — a typical habitat. Lesser whitethroats are found in areas with tall shrub and bush cover and on woodland edges; their song is a tuneless, one-note rattle which may be confused with cirl bunting. Both species are summer visitors to Europe excluding Scandinavia, and the lesser whitethroat is also absent from Italy, Spain and westernmost France, Ireland and northern Britain.

Reed Warbler *Acrocephalus scirpaceus* [illustrated]/**Marsh Warbler**
Acrocephalus palustris L 12.5cm

Reed warblers and marsh warblers look identical — brown above and paler below, with a light stripe over the eye and with no other markings. The reed warbler's song is rather like the sedge warbler's — an even-pitched chatter, 'churr-churr-churr', but with some mimicry. The marsh warbler's performance is more musical and usually mostly mimetic. Reed warblers almost always nest in reed beds, suspending the nest between the stems over water. Marsh warblers breed in many types of tall dense herbage, especially willows or osier thickets with stands of nettles. Both species are summer visitors, reed warblers occurring throughout Europe as far north as southern Scandinavia and England. Marsh warblers are absent from Italy, Spain and southwest France, and very rare in England. The great reed warbler *(Acrocephalus arundinaceus,* L 19cm) is similar but far bigger: it breeds around fresh waters throughout Europe, except the British Isles and Scandinavia, and its song is loud and deliberate with many croaking notes.

Sedge Warbler *Acrocephalus schoenobaenus* 13cm

The sedge warbler's important identification features are the distinct creamy stripe over the eye which makes the head look very flat-crowned, the strongly streaked back and wings, and the plain rufous rump which may be seen when the bird is in flight. The song is a noisy, hurried jumble, including mimicked snatches of other birds' calls and harsh churring as well as quite melodious phrases. It may be delivered from deep cover, but the male also sings during his display flight, rising a few feet from the top of a bush and then gradually descending. Although the song is like that of the reed warbler's, their different appearances separate them. Also, sedge warblers breed in a much wider variety of dense, fairly low vegetation, usually, but not invariably, close to water. They are summer migrants to Europe but do not breed in much of Norway and Sweden or in Spain and southwest France.

Grasshopper Warbler *Locustella naevia* L 13cm

Grasshopper warblers live close to the ground in dense vegetation and so are usually very difficult to see. The song is a high-pitched and even reeling sound, like the ratchet on a fishing-reel, sometimes delivered in short bursts but often continuing for minutes at a time. It is quite distinctive and will carry a long way in calm weather. Even so, locating the bird may be difficult because it turns its head from side to side while singing, and this produces a ventriloquial effect. Often it takes considerable patience to get a good view of the bird which is a fairly uniform olive-brown, with darker streaking on the upperparts and flanks. Their favourite habitat is rank and overgrown meadowland, often close to water but sometimes on dry hillsides and heaths or in woodland clearings. They are summer visitors to western and central Europe but almost absent from Scandinavia except southern Sweden.

Dartford Warbler *Sylvia undata* L 12.5cm

There should be no problem in identifying adult Dartford warblers by their shape and proportions alone. They have small bodies with comparatively large heads, often appearing slightly crested, and long tails often held cocked. Both sexes have dark grey-brown upperparts and pinkish-brown chests, deeper coloured and more heavily speckled with white in the male. Young birds are browner and have shorter tails. Dartford warblers are birds of dry, scrubby country and lowland heath, particularly where there are patches of gorse or even young, scattered pine trees. They are skulking birds and rarely reveal themselves, living on small insects and spiders and with a song rather like that of the whitethroat. They are largely resident in suitable habitats from Italy and Spain through southern and western France into southern England.

Goldcrest *Regulus regulus* L 9cm

Tiny, greenish birds, goldcrests have a distinctive head pattern, consisting of a black line on either side of the crown with a central stripe that is orange in males and yellow in females. Juveniles lack this, but have the same pale double wing bars. Goldcrests are restless, and difficult to watch as they flit through foliage. They have a song like a squeaky little cartwheel and a thin 'see-see-see' call similar to that of treecreepers and tits, and probably serving as a mutually recognizable contact call for their joint winter flocks. Goldcrests live mainly in conifers, although in some areas also in broadleaved woodland, and are resident throughout Europe, except Spain, where they are largely winter visitors. Firecrests *(Regulus ignicapillus)* resemble goldcrests with the addition of black and white eyestripes. They are resident in western and southern areas of Europe, visiting central Europe in summer, but are rare in Britain and absent from Scandinavia.

Willow Warbler *Phylloscopus trochilus* [illustrated]/**Chiffchaff** *Phylloscopus collybita* L 11cm

Both species are rather drab, greenish-brown warblers, almost identical in appearance and best identified by song. Both have dull green backs with a distinct pale stripe above the eye, and pale underparts more or less tinged with yellow. Leg colour is sometimes a guide as chiffchaffs always have dark, blackish legs, but those of willow warblers vary in colour from brown to flesh. The song of the chiffchaff is a repetition of its name in two musical notes, which should not be confused with the great tit's loud 'see-saw'. The willow warbler utters a flowing series of descending notes, often repeated after a short pause. Both species breed in broadleaved woodland and in northern conifer forests; willow warblers are also found in willow and birch scrub. They occur as summer migrants in most of western and northern Europe, and chiffchaffs are resident in southern Europe.

Wood Warbler *Phylloscopus sibilatrix* L 12.5cm

Wood warblers give the impression of being very bright green and yellow — much more so than willow warblers and chiffchaffs — but care must be taken to look for the white belly, as this is the most obvious point of distinction between them and the icterine and melodious warblers. Wood warblers have two different songs, both easily recognized. One consists of repeating the same note, a plaintive whistled 'peeoo', anything up to twenty times. The other commences with a slowly repeated 'stip, stip, stip' and accelerates to a final trill. Wood warblers, like the species they most resemble, feed on insects mainly among the crowns of trees. They are selective in habitat choice, favouring mature beech and oak woods with a fairly open floor. Summer visitors to Europe north to Britain, southern Norway and Sweden, they hardly occur in Ireland or, except on passage, in Spain.

Melodious Warbler *Hippolais polyglotta* L 13cm [illustrated]/Icterine Warbler *Hippolais icterina* L 13.5cm

Both icterine warbler and melodious warblers have a very yellow appearance with greenish backs, yellow eyestripes and completely yellow underparts, unlike the wood warbler which has a white belly. They also have characteristically high foreheads, so that the top of the head appears more pointed than in other warblers. This helps to identify birds in faded plumage. Icterine warblers have pale patches on the wings, which are longer than those of melodious warblers and extend beyond the rump. Both have typical warbler songs, icterine warblers including many discordant notes, and both live in broad-leaved woodland and clumps of trees — icterine warblers in particular feeding in the crowns and needing little ground vegetation. Generally, separating the two species is difficult but fortunately their breeding ranges barely overlap. Melodious warblers are found in Spain and Italy and north into western France. Icterine warblers replace them further north but are absent from Britain and all but southern and western areas of Norway and Sweden.

Siskin *Carduelis spinus* L 12cm

Siskins, serins and greenfinches are all basically greenish and yellow, so care must be taken to distinguish between them. The male siskin has a black crown and chin, yellow underparts, a streaked green back, rather dark wings with conspicuous wing bars, a yellow rump and yellow patches on the sides of the tail. Females and young are browner, more heavily streaked and lack the black crown; the wing and tail markings are much less brilliant yellow but remain the main diagnostic features. They are also smaller than greenfinches which have a comparatively bulky appearance. Siskins feed mainly by extracting seeds from the cones of firs and alders, thus they are seen most often in the treetops, where they are as agile as tits. In winter they often occur in mixed flocks with redpolls. Present all year round in Ireland, Scotland and much of Norway, Sweden and central Europe, siskins usually occur only in winter in southern Britain and other western European countries.

Serin *Serinus serinus* L 11.5cm

The main identification points of this little yellowish finch are the bright yellow rump and lack of wing bars; these distinguish it from both siskin and greenfinch. The male serin has a yellow and green head, yellow breast and rump, and green-brown back and wings. The back and flanks are heavily streaked with dark lines. Females have much less yellow on the head and chest, and juveniles are a rather nondescript streaky brown. The beak is stubbier than in any similar species. Serins are found along woodland edges or in clearings, and in habitats with similar structures such as hedgerows, orchards and gardens. They feed mainly on the seeds of low-growing plants, but also take some tree buds and insects. Primarily birds of the Mediterranean countries, where they occur all year, serins are common migrants further north but in England and Scandinavia they are very rare.

Greenfinch *Carduelis chloris* L 14.5cm

Greenfinches are easily recognized. The male is bright yellow-green, females are slightly duller and juveniles even more so, with faint streaking on the back, but all have clear yellow flashes on the wings and tail. All other greenish finches are more heavily marked by dark streaking, while the size and build, notched tail and heavy, seed-eater's beak, remove any risk of confusion with the smaller and delicate insectivorous warblers. Yellow wagtails are even brighter yellow, with much longer tails, and yellowhammers have brown backs and chestnut rumps. Greenfinches are found in open woodland, along hedges with trees or tall bushes and often in suburban gardens and parks. In spring, they have a loud and rather nasal 'dzw-e-e' call. Feeding mainly on seeds and buds, they are resident throughout Europe as far north as southern Norway and Sweden, occurring further north only as summer migrants.

Crossbill *Loxia curvirostra* L 16.5cm

A rather stout, large-headed finch, the crossbill's most unusual feature is its beak, a specialized tool with which the bird can prise up the scales of fir cones and extract the seeds. Adult males are deep red and females are dark greenish, but immatures may be streaky brownish or may have some red on them. Crossbills are found particularly in spruce woods throughout Scandinavia and in many sorts of conifers over much of eastern and central Europe, Spain, Scotland and eastern England. When the population reaches a high level, birds 'erupt' and many overwinter and sometimes stay to breed all over Europe. In Norway and Sweden two similar species occur. The parrot crossbill *(Loxia pytyopsittacus)* is almost identical, but has a heavier beak for feeding on pine cones. The pine grosbeak *(Pinicola enucleator)* breeds in birch and conifer woods and has a double wing bar. Elsewhere, crossbills are unlikely to be confused with other species as their feeding methods and habitat are distinctive.

Goldfinch *Carduelis carduelis* L 12cm

Among the most easily recognized birds, male and female goldfinches are practically identical. The yellow flashes on blackish wings show up brilliantly, especially when the birds are in their very bouncing and erratic flight. Young birds are greyish buff, streaked with brown, but also have yellow wings. Goldfinches live where trees provide nest-sites and cover, while adjoining open ground offers feeding places. They feed almost entirely on plant seeds and are particularly associated with thistles, their beaks being long and narrow enough to extract the seed from the tough heads. The male's bill is longer than the female's and thus he can feed on seeds that she cannot easily reach: this probably increases the survival rate of both sexes when food is short. Goldfinches are present throughout the year in almost all of Europe except the east, and Norway and Sweden, where they occur only in summer.

Linnet *Acanthis cannabina* L 13.5cm

In spring, the male linnet has a red crown and breast, greyish head and a rich chestnut back. By autumn, the colours are duller and more like females or juveniles, which are brown above and fawn below, streaked with darker marks, but lighter coloured than redpolls. Another important point of distinction is the white bar on the edge of every linnet's folded wing, which shows in flight as a light patch on the outer wing. Linnets inhabit open areas with bushes or low trees and feed mainly on the seeds of low-growing plants. They are resident throughout western Europe, and migratory on the northern edge of their range in Scandinavia where they are largely replaced, as in upland Britain and Ireland, by twites *(Acanthis flavirostris)*: these resemble hen linnets, except that the males develop pink rumps in summer. In winter many twites move to the coast, especially salt marshes, where they occur in flocks.

Redpoll *Acanthis flammea* L 14cm

Redpolls are basically brownish finches and may be confused with linnets. The key distinction is that all adult redpolls have a small, black patch below the beak. Each also has a deep red crown patch throughout the year, unlike male linnets which lose theirs in autumn. Breeding males have pink breasts, but at other seasons resemble the females, whose chests are fawn, streaked with brown. Scandinavian breeding birds have whitish rumps, but those that breed in the British Isles have uniform brown, streaked upper parts. The feeding zones of redpolls are different from those of linnets. Redpolls live mainly on tree seeds, especially those of conifers, alder and birch and take weed seeds relatively infrequently. Present all year in the British Isles, parts of Scandinavia and central European mountains, redpolls are summer visitors to northern Scandinavia, and in winter may be found as far south as the Mediterranean coast.

Bullfinch *Pyrrhula pyrrhula* L 15cm

The cock bullfinch's red front, black cap and white wing bar are an easily recognized combination. The female has a dull pinkish chest but otherwise resembles the male; juveniles are brownish and without the black caps. All bullfinches are plump, thick-necked birds and have stout, conical beaks which they use to feed largely on tree buds and seeds. In the eastern part of their range they are particularly associated with conifers, but in western Europe they also live in broadleaved woodland, orchards and other bushy cover. In flight, bullfinches display a white rump which contrasts with the greyish back and black tail: this is often the only view you get as the bird slips away through the trees. They form much smaller winter flocks than other finches. Bullfinches are resident over most of western Europe except northern Scandinavia, where some birds are migratory, and Spain where they mainly occur in winter.

Chaffinch *Fringilla coelebs* L 15cm

Both male and female chaffinches have two distinct white bars on each wing, very evident in flight and at rest, so that even in deep woodland shade the species is usually easily identified. Unlike bramblings, the male's markings are the same at all seasons — bluish head, pink face and chest, rich brown back and greenish rump. Females have grey-green upperparts with a paler breast and belly. Chaffinches are common and widespread finches. In the breeding season they occur in all sorts of woodland, feeding on insects, and at other seasons they live on seeds picked up from the ground. In most of Norway, Sweden and in eastern Europe chaffinches are present only in summer, but elsewhere they may be found throughout the year. Often winter flocks can be seen feeding within woodland or on open ground, and in some areas these tend to be composed of birds of the same sex.

Brambling *Fringilla montifringilla* L 14.5cm

The overall impression of an orange, black and white finch makes the brambling fairly distinctive, and the long white patch on the rump is a good clue to the bird's identity in flight. The male has a black head and back only in the summer. After the autumn moult it looks like a brightly coloured female or juvenile, with buffish head and back, orange breast and shoulders, white rump and black tail. However, the cock's new head and back feathers are actually buff only at the tips, and wear down to reveal the black beneath, so that the change into breeding plumage does not require another energy-consuming moult. Breeding across much of Scandinavia in birch, open conifer woods and high willow scrub, bramblings feed on seeds and insects. In winter they move south and occur throughout Europe, concentrating on areas where food, notably beechmast, is temporarily plentiful.

Ortolan Bunting *Emberiza hortulana* L 16.5cm

The male ortolan bunting has a greenish-grey hood overlain by yellow markings on the lower face and throat. The back is brown and the underparts are a rich pinkish-buff, unlike the yellow belly of both the yellowhammer and the cirl bunting. Females are duller, with streaking in the area of the hood, and buff face and throat marks conforming to the same pattern as in the male. Both have a distinct light eye ring and this is a noticeable feature of the immature birds. Ortolan buntings are birds of open country and farmland with a few trees. They are present in Europe only in summer, when they are widespread in eastern Europe, but have a somewhat patchy distribution in the west, being largely absent from parts of Iberia and from northern France, the Low Countries, Denmark and much of Norway. A very few occur in Britain on migration but do not breed.

Yellowhammer *Emberiza citrinella* L 16.5cm

With a predominantly yellow head and underparts, contrasting with a rich brown back, the male yellowhammer is unlikely to be mistaken for any other species. The yellow wagtail has quite a different build and behaviour. Female and young yellowhammers are less yellow, and confusion with female and juvenile cirl buntings is possible; however, in flight all yellowhammers reveal a strikingly bright chestnut rump. The male usually sings from the top of a bush, repeating a simple phrase, 'chwi-chwi-chwi-chwi-chwi-chwee'. Yellowhammers are widespread and common birds, living on the edges of woodland, in young plantations or open country provided there are hedges or scrub patches. In winter they sometimes form flocks with finches. They are largely resident throughout Europe but in the extreme north of Norway and Sweden they occur as summer migrants, and in much of Spain and the Mediterranean coastal zone are present only in winter.

Cirl Bunting *Emberiza cirlus* L 16.5cm

The strongly contrasting head and face markings of the male cirl bunting form a distinctive and easily recognized pattern — the dark crown and throat in particular separating this species from the yellowhammer. Females and juveniles of both species are very similar — brown above and dull yellow below with speckled heads, backs and flanks. They are best separated by rump colour, which is olive in the cirl bunting and bright rufous in the yellowhammer; female ortolan buntings and young birds have brown rumps and a distinctive light eye ring. The male cirl bunting's song is uninspired — a brief rattle on one note, rather like that of the lesser whitethroat. Seeming to like much the same habitat as yellowhammers, although perhaps with a greater affinity for situations including trees as well as bushes, cirl buntings are resident west and south of a line running roughly from southern England across northern France and southern Germany to Greece.

Reed Bunting *Emberiza schoeniclus* L 15cm

The male reed bunting is easy to identify, having a black head and throat, the two parts separated by a white diagonal running from the beak to the white nape. The back is rich brown and the underparts are pale. In winter the head is browner but at all seasons the simple, contrasting pattern is very striking. Young males have indistinct head and throat markings and females are much duller with a brownish head, relieved mainly by a white line forming a distinct V under the cheek, and a dark moustachial stripe. Adults and young alike have dark tails, with white outer margins which are very evident in flight. Reed buntings are mainly found in marshy habitats but recently, in some areas, they have colonized the drier situations associated with yellowhammers. They are present all year throughout western Europe including the British Isles and southern Scandinavia, but in the rest of Norway and Sweden occur only in summer.

House Sparrow *Passer domesticus* L 14.5cm

House sparrows are so common in proximity to man that everyone must know them, but it is as well to be sure of their particular features in order to be confident of correctly identifying species which look somewhat similar. The male has a grey crown and more or less black bib, with a pale cheek and a distinct white wing bar. Hens and juveniles are rather drab, light brown birds, with a darker crown and a stripe through the eye, streaked backs and comparatively pale underparts. Closely associated with human settlement, house sparrows normally nest in holes, often in buildings, but will take over the nestholes of other birds or even build in ivy or hedgerows. Although basically seed eaters, house sparrows have learned to take a wide range of the other foods made available by man: in later summer many urban birds move into the fields to exploit the ripe grain. They are a resident species in almost every European region.

Tree Sparrow *Passer montanus* L 14cm

Rather a trim and smart little bird by comparison with the often scruffy house sparrow, the tree sparrow is distinguished by its chestnut crown and the black mark on its cheek, as well as by a smaller black bib than in the related species. Adults and young birds are alike. Their calls are higher pitched and crisper than those of house sparrow — a short 'chik, chik', and a characteristic flight note, 'tek, tek'. Essentially birds of open woodland and areas with scattered trees, tree sparrows are a much more rural species than house sparrows. They are hole nesters, usually selecting sites in trees and rarely using situations in buildings. Tree sparrows are resident over much of Europe. In Ireland they are now confined to a limited coastal zone and in Britain, although common in the lowlands, they are thinly distributed in many upland areas. They are summer migrants to north Norway and absent from Sweden.

Corn Bunting *Emberiza calandra* L 18cm

Corn buntings achieve distinction by an almost complete lack of any unusual features. The head, back and rump are light brown, and evenly marked with darker streaks; the underparts are buff with brown spotting on the chest, sometimes creating a necklace effect. The stout beak and lack of any crest, wing bar or light feathers in the tail also serve to separate them from larks and pipits. The sexes are similar and have a somewhat bulky, heavy look, sometimes flying with legs dangling. The song is a high-pitched, breathless jangle. Birds of open country including arable farmland, corn buntings feed on the ground and normally use low perches, although they have taken well to telephone wires. They are resident throughout Europe except in Norway and the extreme south of Sweden; in Britain they are absent from the uplands but present in suitable lowland areas. In Ireland they are confined to coastal situations.

Meadow Pipit *Anthus pratensis* L 14.5cm [middle]/**Tree Pipit** *Anthus trivialis* L 15cm/**Rock Pipit** *Anthus spinoletta* L 16.5cm [bottom]

At first glance, most pipits look like a cross between larks and thrushes, but there are several obvious points of difference. Related to wagtails, pipits have a similar sleek look with an often rather horizontal stance and longish tails which they flick frequently. They walk and run on the ground rather than creeping like larks or hopping like thrushes. They are also smaller than thrushes and have streaked upperparts and crowns, as well as light outer tail feathers; although the skylark shares these features, pipits are slimmer birds without crests.

Meadow pipits and tree pipits are hard to distinguish from each other except by breeding habitat, behaviour and voice. Tree pipits usually nest in grassland or heath with scattered trees, or in open woods. Meadow pipits prefer completely open grass or moorland. Both species have song flights, rising to no great height and then fluttering down; the tree pipit often starts and finishes from a perch, and will also sing from the tree tops, but meadow pipits rarely perch in trees. Both have a very much briefer and more repetitive song than skylarks, the tree pipit's often ending in a carrying 'seea-seea-seea'. Tree pipits are summer visitors to Europe excluding Ireland and most of Spain, and meadow pipits are summer visitors to Norway and Sweden, resident in central and western Europe including Ireland, and winter visitors to the south.

Rock pipits breed on rocky shores from France and the British Isles northwards, and winter on all coasts between Denmark and Spain. They are darker coloured than meadow pipits or tree pipits, with dark grey legs and grey outer tail feathers, whereas meadow pipits' and tree pipits' legs are flesh coloured and their outer tail feathers are white. Scandinavian rock pipits are brownish above and below, but those that live in the south are distinctly greyish.

Skylark *Alauda arvensis* L 18cm

Skylarks are best known for their song flights, the males rising vertically, often to great height to hover and then descend, producing throughout a loud and musical song. This is easily learned and distinguished from those of other birds which have song flights, such as meadow pipits. Birds of open country, skylarks almost never perch in trees — unlike the rather similar woodlarks and tree pipits. Neither woodlarks nor another similar species, the crested lark, have the wholly white outer tail feathers so easily seen on the skylark. Standing on a wall or alert on the ground, perhaps with the crest erect, skylarks look quite different from the dumpy, crouching forms they present when feeding on the ground. They are resident over much of Europe, but most Scandinavian birds move south in winter, and in other regions birds may leave their breeding grounds to flock where food is abundant.

Woodlark *Lullua arborea* L 15cm

Woodlarks show a number of features which distinguish them from other larks and pipits. Given a good view, it will be possible to see that the eyestripes meet at the back of the head, that there is a black-and-white mark on the wing edge, and that the tail has a white tip. The tail is also rather short and makes the bird look somewhat bat-like in the air. The song is very mellow and liquid, and often delivered while the bird rises and flies along a looping path between the tops of two bushes. Woodlarks live in country with scattered trees and shrubs, such as heath and parkland, and on the edges of woods. Resident and largely sedentary in southern and western Europe, their range extends north to southern England and Denmark, and they appear as summer visitors in southern Sweden and most of eastern Europe.

Crested Lark *Galerida cristata* L 17cm

Usually there should be no difficulty in identifying the crested lark which, as its name implies, has an obvious crest that is usually held erect. There is no white on the tail, the outer feathers being orange-brown. The song somewhat resembles that of the skylark, but it is usually delivered from the ground or a perch and the song flight does not compare with the skylarks performance. The flight call is trisyllabic, a liquid 'wee-wee-ooo' quite unlike the short 'chirrup' of the skylark. Crested larks are resident over all of Europe (except the British Isles), and most of Norway and Sweden. They are particularly associated with dry, dusty and sandy areas where there are patches of bare ground and short vegetation. They occur frequently in industrial settings such as railway yards and waste ground, as well as in village streets and town suburbs.

Pied Wagtail [illustrated]/**White Wagtail** *Motacilla alba* L 18cm

The pied wagtail is resident in the British Isles whereas white wagtails breed throughout the rest of Europe, being migratory in Germany, northern France, the Low Countries and Scandinavia; some occur in Britain on passage. In the breeding season the male pied wagtail has black upperparts and breast contrasting with a white face, belly and white wing bars. The female is similar except that she has a dark grey back. Both sexes are less strongly pied in winter. White wagtails are usually much paler birds than pied wagtails, with light grey backs and wings. One sure point of distinction between adults of the two races is that pied wagtails have black rumps and white wagtails' rumps are grey. All young birds are brownish, usually with a vestigial throat patch.

Grey Wagtail *Motacilla cinerea* L 18cm

All wagtails are sleek and restless birds, and none more so than the grey wagtail with its exceptionally long tail, constantly in motion. Both sexes have a grey crown and back, yellow underparts and a black tail with white edges. In summer, cock birds have neat black bibs. Juveniles may be paler, brownish on the back and fawn beneath but, like the adults, they have bright yellow hindquarters which are very evident and provide a good identification mark as the bird flies away. More closely associated with running water than the related species, grey wagtails hunt for insects along clear, fast-flowing streams, running swiftly along the margins and also catching flies in flight over the water's surface. They are a largely resident species, occurring along suitable water courses throughout Europe including the British Isles north to southern Denmark. A few breed as summer migrants in southern Sweden.

Yellow Wagtail [illustrated]/**Blue-headed Wagtail** *Motacilla flava* L 16.5cm

Several races of yellow wagtail breed in different parts of Europe. The main distinction between them is in the head markings of the males. All adults have completely yellow underparts and greenish backs. Females' heads are also greenish. Most males occurring in Britain have very yellow heads and can look as bright as canaries. In southern Scandinavia and central Europe the males have bluish crowns and cheeks, with a distinct pale eyestripe; in northern Scandinavia the crown and cheeks are uniformly dark grey and the back is darker green. Care must be taken to distinguish this species from the grey wagtail whose back is truly grey and whose tail is much longer. Summer visitors to all of Europe except Ireland and the north and west of Britain, where they are very rare, yellow wagtails breed in wet grasslands, usually in proximity to water.

Index

Figures in italic type refer
to the species description
with accompanying colour
illustration.